S0-AFF-509

materials

architecture in detail

edited by oscar riera ojeda

introduction and captions by mark pasnik

chapter headings by james mccown

photography by paul warchol

© 2003 by Rockport Publishers, Inc.

All rights reserved. No part of this book may be reproduced in any form without written permission of the copyright owners. All images in this book have been reproduced with the knowledge and prior consent of the artists concerned, and no responsibility is accepted by producer, publisher, or printer for any infringement of copyright or otherwise, arising from the contents of this publication. Every effort has been made to ensure that credits accurately comply with information supplied.

First published in the United States of America by Rockport Publishers, Inc.
33 Commercial Street
Gloucester, Massachusetts 01930-5089
Telephone: (978) 282-9590
Fax: (978) 283-2742
www.rockpub.com

Library of Congress Cataloging-in-Publication data available.

design by oscar riera ojeda and lucas guerra

layout by oscar riera ojeda

ISBN 1-56496-930-4

10 9 8 7 6 5 4 3 2 1

Manufactured in China by Palace Press International.

Cover: Olson Sundberg Kundig Allen Architects, Mission Hill Family Estate Winery, Westbank, British Columbia, Canada, 2001. Previous page: Davis Brody Bond, University Hall Residence, New York University, New York, 1998. This spread: Steven Holl Architects, Chapel of St. Ignatius, Seattle, 1997. Contents page: Maya Lin Studio/David Hotson Architect, Upper East Side Residence, New York, 1999.

Back flap photography credits: portraits of Mark Pasnik and Oscar Riera Ojeda © Lisa Pascarelli (top) and Paul Warchol © Abraham Aronow (bottom).

rockport publishers

contents

introduction by mark pasnik

Delicate or weighty, machined or handcrafted, opulent or sterile, precise or roughshod, dynamic or staid, weathered or timeless—much of contemporary architecture seems to underscore one of the obsessions of many architects practicing today: a transfixion with details. But the obsession is more than mere intoxication; it reflects a complex view of the detail's relationship to craft and to fabrication, combined with an understanding of details as communicators of ideas and as material expressions of an architect's authorship. ■ It is in light of this condition that Oscar Riera Ojeda and I have set out to create a new series of books focused on the detail's role in shaping and defining architecture. Through the conduit of *Architecture in Detail*, we plan to examine the work of a number of the profession's most engaging contemporary designers. Each book will center on a theme, beginning here with *Materials*, immediately followed by *Elements*, with still others planned for the future. The topics are rich and ever-changing, precisely because the detail is such a powerful force in architecture's ability to speak to us—a force that has been shaped by a number of factors over its evolving history. ■ Details can be many things in architecture. Most literally, they are taken to be the pieces of a building that need to be studied, drawn, and communicated by an architect to a builder. At this basest of

word, an "autographing" of the building.[2] The works presented in this volume are small-scale signatures of each designer, an autographing that, as we shall see, relies heavily upon the expressive capacity of materials to achieve powerful architectural effects. ■ The detail's modern history has undergone great scrutiny in the last decade with such works as Kenneth Frampton's *Studies in Tectonic Culture* or Edward Ford's *The Details of Modern Architecture*. Dissatisfaction with the contemporary state of the architectural avant-garde may in part underlie this reawakened fascination with the modern detail. In the face of globalization and digitized architecture, many architects and critics ascribe to a phenomenological view of details as counter-products, symbols of a return to more human architectural dimensions in contrast to the head-spinning, blob-like forms produced by today's computer generation. Details are often described in poetic terms, as tectonic expressions of joinery or structure, or as evidence of architecture's link to a sense of craft produced by the human hand. Such a position breeds nostalgia for craft's authenticity, for an architectural ideology that weighs the particular over the universal, the natural over the machined. Yet in fact, craft's authenticity was compromised long ago by the competing restraints of economics and construction practices. ■ One example

the material autograph

readings, the drawn detail serves a translational function—"a moment where the design idea engages the material reality of built form" in the words of the editors of *Praxis*, a journal that itself seeks to accomplish this very task.[1] A detail straddles many worlds: it is the idea, it is the drawing, and it is the built product. ■ So too, there is a sense of individuality to the detail. It is drawn because it is unique, because it requires special instruction for its implementation, because it is not practice as usual. For some, the detail's distinctiveness also implies that it is unrepeatable, but in our era of mechanical reproduction, the drawn detail might just as well be repeated endlessly. No matter which is the case, details are drawn because they differ from standard construction techniques. They are moments of originality, expressed in the voice of the particular author. Thus details are often the closest connection between architect and building—and the most intimate sign of the architect's authorship. They are, to use Carlo Scarpa's

of this is evident in the influences of the nineteenth century's reaction to the rising tide of the Industrial Revolution. Mid-century critics such as John Ruskin and William Morris led a moralistic critique against mechanization's degrading effects on the qualities of both products and architecture. Historian Nikolaus Pevsner recounts Morris's scornful view that "practically all industrial art was crude."[3] This disdain for machined production eventually led to the Arts and Crafts movement in Britain and the United States of the late nineteenth century, which proposed to reintegrate art and life by returning craft to the forefront of aesthetic morality. Nothing less than "a revival of artistic craftsmanship"[4] was envisioned, resulting in such works of delicately crafted expressions as Charles and Henry Greene's Gamble House in Pasadena, California of the early twentieth century [figures 1–2]. Here, iron straps or wooden pegs and wedges make visual its process of handcrafted assembly. And yet this example embodies a deception, in which the visible assembly often masks the actual joinery systems composed of modern fasteners. While perhaps sidestepping purist Arts and Crafts ideals, Greene and Greene's work introduced the idea of representation into the vocabulary of craft. Craft could be *expressed*, not simply demonstrated.[5] And as a consequence, its veneer of purist authenticity came into question. ■ In contrast to Morris's vilification, the modern movement fully embraced machinery, but did so at times with parallel aspirations for craft. The Deutscher Werkbund, for instance, pursued the ideal of *Qualität* through the control of mass production techniques, rather than through refined handcraftsmanship. In other words, by harnessing the machine, details no longer required the presence of the hand to be rich sources of craft. Yet despite early modernism's investment in the importance of details as expressions of quality, by the mid-twentieth century, modernist values had shifted dramatically toward more purely functionalist concerns. The detail had again become lifeless, moribund, stiffly functional. It took the rising careers in the 1950s of two central figures, Carlo Scarpa and Louis Kahn, to return architecture "to the idea of craft, construction method, and on-site invention as the ultimate creative acts."[6] ■ Scarpa's work, in particular, centered on the detail as a moment of communication between the architect and the

sophisticated details, to our contemporary eye the total immersion in the artisan's process appears perhaps nostalgic, even unrealistic in light of today's building practices. The presumption of an artistic alliance between a master architect and a master artisan seems equally contrived for an industry in which teams of designers and manufacturers and trades people are necessary to construct a building.[7] Yet this book's collection of work does not lament the loss of collaborative craft, nor does it fall back to the lifelessness of the machine era, nor even the detail-bereft world of cyber-architecture. Instead, in the face of mass production and consumer culture, it turns appropriately enough to material expression. In some sense, materials have become a surrogate to craft in these works, a surrogate that establishes an architectural voice that is humane in its tactility and modern in its production. ■ This is not to say that the details shown in this book are poorly executed. In fact, nothing could be further from the truth. Their tactility simply has replaced the hand-worn richness of the craftsman's art. Thus, many of these projects reinvent a modernity that spans the precision of the old modernism and the spirit of something handmade. Their material nature infuses vibrancy into the rigor of the modern era, while capitalizing on the enthralling lushness of the ever-expanding possibilities of new fabrication methods. ■ In each of these details, the

artisan. His process of design evolved based upon the intense input of his fabricators. Craft thus occupied Scarpa's design process in ways that were both personal and collaborative, with results that paralleled the strokes of a painter's brush or the imprint of a sculptor's fingers; there remains in the final object a distinct mark of its creator. Here, the machine era's distance between designer and built product is corrected by the collaboration between architect and artisan, in a shared effort to maximize craft. Consequently, Scarpa's projects host an array of refined fabrications and techniques—from the horizontal banding of board-formed concrete to the delicate integration of stone, glass tiles, and brass pieces [figures 3–5]. His building process was research-driven; the limitations of a craft informed the design, and the design in turn reshaped those limitations by testing the potentials of various construction processes. ■ Clearly the works gathered here differ in this aspiration. If we may admire Scarpa's buildings for their

qualities of craft persist. We see architects who detail with an insistence on honesty of materials, as Louis Kahn did, building on what a material "wants" to be. Others take the reverse approach, and test the way in which materials can be pushed beyond their limits or be placed in unfamiliar contexts. Some designers focus on materials in their relation to one another and their ability to produce effects in tandem. Others use raw or inelegant materials elegantly. Some experiment with unconventional construction processes, using materials in new ways, while others co-opt materials not traditionally associated with architecture. ■ This array of material techniques enriches our experience of each building. Pattern, for instance, takes varied forms in these works. Architecture Research Office's SoHo Loft in New York [pages 74–75] uses the veining of deep blue Bahia granite panels that are book-matched to create a highly figured surface around which the activities of the loft are arranged. Contrast this to Steven Holl's Cranbrook

Institute of Science [pages 188–189], where light passes through mottled glass, casting prismatic colors and refractions on what are otherwise spare plaster surfaces. The latter involves outwardly projecting the pattern of a transparent material, the former visually draws us deeply into the pattern of a solid. ■ In ARO's Colorado House, the repetition of cor-ten shingles gives texture to a series of parallel organizing walls [pages 82–83]; as the metal surfaces slip into the house, they counterbalance the smoothness of plaster and polished concrete. A perforated copper skin sheathes Steven Holl's Sarphatistraat Offices [pages 86–87] in a pattern based upon the repetitive puncturing of continuous metal plates. The skin provides a screened space for light between its inner and outer layers. Such details are expressive evocations of both the material's characteristics and the mechanical processes of fabrication that shaped it. ■ Each material has within it a range of uses, some conventional, others unexpected. Peter Marino's Chanel Store in Osaka, Japan, is composed of a low-iron, clear glass curtain wall with a white ceramic interlayer and complemented by panels of acid-etched mirrored glass [pages 182–183]. The building reads by day as a white cube, while at night the LED backlighting enlivens its surfaces with theatrical displays. A similarly milky, backlit glass serves a very different function in a staircase at the USM Furniture

Parallam pieces, a product typically used in structural applications. In both Holl's project and Helfand's, the comparison is enriched not only by the differences in the materials' inherent qualities, but also by contrasting techniques of fabrication. In one, ordinary mass-produced blocks frame unique, poured glass figures; in the other, panels manufactured from glue-laminated wood fibers are set against uniformly processed plastic. ■ Perhaps even more remarkable than such contrasts is the relentlessness of material uniformity. Craig Bassam's Bally Store in Berlin [pages 30–33] employs a standard Swiss flooring product of fine-grained European oak across its many wall, floor, and stair surfaces. Ironically, the effect's complexity is dependent upon its rigorous consistency, where the material was precisely laid out by a cabinetmaker. Joints between surfaces are visually foregrounded because the material subtly responds to the store's three-dimensional terrain. Similarly, the wooden surface in Rem Koolhaas's Prada Store in SoHo [pages 158–159] changes from floor to staircase to theatrical seating to a ramping sine wave. The detail's material continuity cloaks a variety of conditions beneath a blanket of exotic zebrawood. ■ It is, however, not entirely surprising that contemporary architectural details should have such open-ended freedoms. After all, many of the looming figures of the twentieth century depended heavily upon the power of material details to fully

Showroom in New York by MSM Architects [pages 174–177]. The stair's structural supports are concealed behind four layers of half-inch, low-iron glass with a translucent plastic interlayer. Its steps are detached four inches from the sidewalls of tempered glass, such that the staircase appears to be a free-floating, crystalline form. There is no evidence of handicraft and no striving for honesty of material connections here; the stair's beauty relies upon details that promote other impressions. ■ A common strategy for adding richness to a project is seen in the juxtaposition of materials. Steven Holl's Stretto House in Dallas [pages 52–53] contrasts the supple fluidity of cast glass forms with the rigid march of concrete blocks assembled in a running bond. The design of Helfand Architecture's offices for DoubleClick in New York [pages 156–157] centers on the interplay of inexpensive industrial materials that include corrugated plastic wall panels supported by aluminum angle frames. Tables and cabinetry are formed from heavy-grained

form their architectural vocabulary. Scarpa, as we have seen already, wedded history and the present in joinery details that unify artifacts with interventions, across materials and across times. His materials engage one another—at the same time that they engage us. Louis Kahn's monumentalism was advanced in his decisions at the smallest of scales. Kahn's noble concretes, travertines, and woods were meant to absorb the long-term effects of weather as well as the pace of natural light flowing across their surfaces [figures 6–8]. Frank Lloyd Wright's natural materials were detailed with connections between outside and inside worlds, reaffirming his organic principles and his attempt to dissolve boundaries between the natural and the architectural. To represent his structural agenda, Ludwig Mies van der Rohe mounted precise columnar details to his façades; their materials were machined, but with a luscious elegance writ in bronzes and chromes uncommon to the actual aesthetic of machines [figures 9–11]. Each of these members of the modern pantheon enlisted—and was dependent upon—materials to support a particular philosophical approach. ■ Contemporary details show an expansion of these possibilities and an even greater capacity to infuse material life into a building's details. The romantic notion of craft may be to some extent absent from our world today, but its effects, its character, and its emotion remain visible in the analogous vitality of materials. This condition recalls a text by the Italian modernist architect Luigi Moretti. He wrote of art's most significant force, the quality of "condensing reality." Art is "a representation," one that "must release a density of energy very superior to real life."[8] Moretti identified this notion of density in the profiles of stone moldings. Such elements, in his view, represented more than their material quality; they were signs of the forces of a building, the forces between wall and ceiling. Among the details on the pages to follow, the earthbound realness of the material is complemented by a similar characteristic to this density of art. Physical features are only half the effect. These details rise to something greater in their explorations, in the patterns they project or absorb, in their richness or austerity or deception. The projects fully embrace their material capacity to transform, to be shaped by light, to affect our senses. And as a consequence, these works offer an *extra*-material voice that is the architect's signature. Le Corbusier invoked this added presence in his writings: "One

Notes

1. Ashley Schafer and Amanda Reeser, "Defining Detail," *Praxis*, issue 1 (2000), 4. ■ 2. Nicholas Olsberg, "Introduction," *Carlo Scarpa Architect: Intervening with History* (New York: The Monacelli Press, 1992), 13. ■ 3. Nikolaus Pevsner, *Pioneers of Modern Design* (New York: Penguin Books, 1978), 20. ■ 4. *ibid.*, 25. ■ 5. Edward R. Ford, *The Details of Modern Architecture* (Cambridge, MA: MIT Press, 1994), 143–151. ■ 6. George Ranalli, "History, Craft, Invention," *Carlo Scarpa Architect: Intervening with History* (New York: The Monacelli Press, 1992), 40. ■ 7. Peggy Deamer, "Detail: The Subject of the Object," *Praxis*, issue 1 (2000), 108–115. ■ 8. Luigi Moretti, "The Values of Profiles," *Oppositions*, vol. 4 (October, 1974), 116. ■ 9. Le Corbusier, *Towards a New Architecture* (New York: Dover Publications, 1986), 153. ■ 10. Peter Zumthor, *Kunsthaus Bregenz* (Ostfildern, Germany: Hatje Cantz, 1999), 13.

9

10

uses stone, wood, cement, and turns them into houses or palaces; that's construction. It calls for skill. But suddenly you touch my heart; you make me feel good. I am happy. I say: it's beautiful. This is architecture. It is art."[9] ■ But perhaps the idea of a material art is as overly romantic as the nineteenth century's insistence on a return to craft. Architect Peter Zumthor challenges us to see beauty from an alternative viewpoint. In describing his *Kunsthaus* in Bregenz, he writes that "the building is exactly what we see and touch, exactly what we feel beneath our feet: a cast concrete, stony body."[10] Could these details be defined as just that, a material taking on a life of its own? Could they partly receive their strength from exactly what they are? Could they principally be receptors for our eyes, our hands, our feet—is this not central to the material legacy?

Image Captions and Credits

Figures 1–2: Charles and Henry Greene, Gamble House, Pasadena, California, 1908; images courtesy Doug Dolezal. ■ Figures 3–5: Carlo Scarpa, Brion Family Tomb, San Vito d'Altivole, Italy, 1978; images courtesy Doug Dolezal. ■ Figures 6–8: Louis Kahn, Kimbell Art Museum, Fort Worth, Texas, 1972; Salk Institute for Biological Studies, La Jolla, California, 1965; images courtesy Doug Dolezal. ■ Figures 9–11: Ludwig Mies van der Rohe, Seagram Building, New York, 1958; images by Paul Warchol.

wood

"Wood is the most humanly intimate of all materials," said Frank Lloyd Wright. ■ "Man loves his association with it, likes to feel it under his hand, sympathetic to his touch and to his eye." ■ Originally scorned by modernists as insufficiently attuned to their machine aesthetic, wood only gradually entered the twentieth century designers' repertoire. ■ Timeless and primeval, wood can soften the hard edges of steel and glass. ■ In wood's multiple striations, we see intimations of our own mortality, in its infinitely variable grain patterns, we see artistry by nature itself.

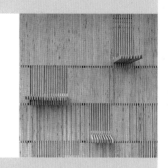

Previous spread: Craig Konyk, Graduate Architecture Student Installation, Parsons School of Design, New York, 1995. This spread: Brian Healy Architects (with Michael Ryan), Beach House, Loveladies, New Jersey, 1997. Horizontal wooden slats provide protection from the morning sun in the principal living spaces of the house, contained within a glass pavilion.

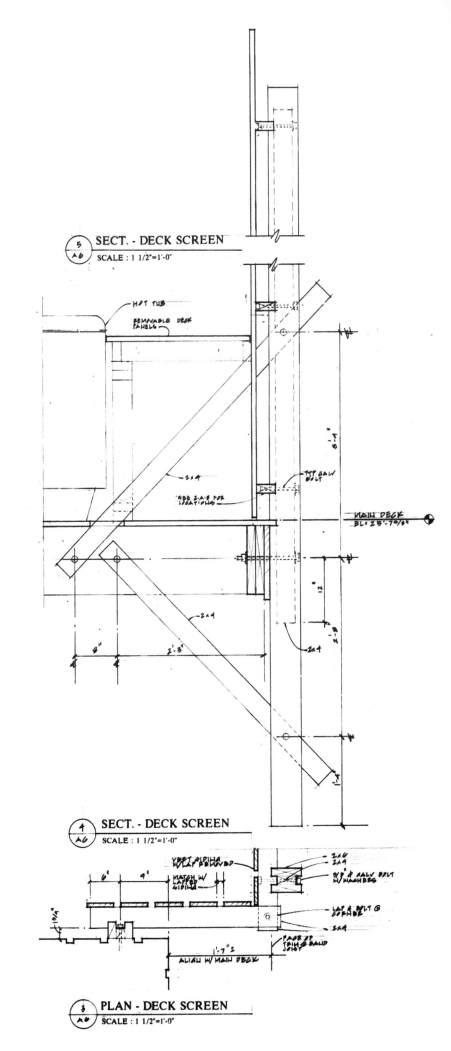

5 SECT. - DECK SCREEN
A6 SCALE : 1 1/2"=1'-0"

4 SECT. - DECK SCREEN
A6 SCALE : 1 1/2"=1'-0"

3 PLAN - DECK SCREEN
A6 SCALE : 1 1/2"=1'-0"

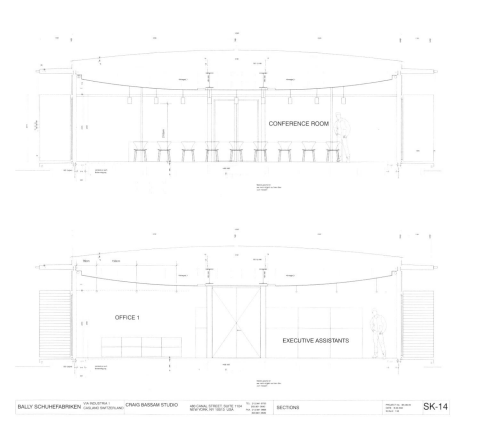

BALLY SCHUHEFABRIKEN | VIA INDUSTRIA 1 CASLANO SWITZERLAND | CRAIG BASSAM STUDIO | 480 CANAL STREET, SUITE 1104 NEW YORK, NY 10013 USA | TEL. 212.941.9700 212.801.0840 FAX. 212.941.9866 203.801.0839 | SECTIONS | PROJECT No. SK-06.00 DATE. 8.00.1000 SCALE. 1:50 | SK-14

CONFERENCE ROOM

OFFICE 1

EXECUTIVE ASSISTANTS

Craig Bassam Studio, Bally Caslano Headquarters, Caslano, Switzerland, 2000. A pavilion housing offices and a showroom was added to the roof of an existing concrete factory, and its modularly constructed platform, walls, screens, and soffits are wrapped in sealed solid oak.

Nader Tehrani with Kristen Giannattasio and Heather Walls, *Immaterial/Ultramaterial: Thin-Ply*, Harvard Graduate School of Design, Cambridge, Massachusetts, 2001. Drawing from apparel design, this installation incorporates darts in thin-ply sapele mahogany to give volume to a flat surface, seamlessly navigating between a hung ceiling, a bowed truss, and a column wrap.

Steven Holl Architects, Cranbrook Institute of Science, Bloomfield Hills, Michigan, 1999. The lobby materials include perforated plywood panels, textured concrete walls, as well as brushed metal handrails and door pulls. Following spread: Steven Holl Architects, Chapel of St. Ignatius, Seattle, 1997. The chapel's Alaskan yellow cedar doors were hand carved and are highlighted by cast bronze handles.

Gluckman Mayner Architects, Katayone Adeli Boutique, New York, 1999. The texture of a new tin ceiling counterbalances the purity of abstracted volumes. Constructed of plywood panels, display surfaces are stained black and sealed with polyurethane.

Gabellini Associates, Rosenblat Jewelry Showroom and Atelier, Hamburg, Germany, 1998. American walnut treads and risers appear to be notched into the plaster wall in this serpentine stair.

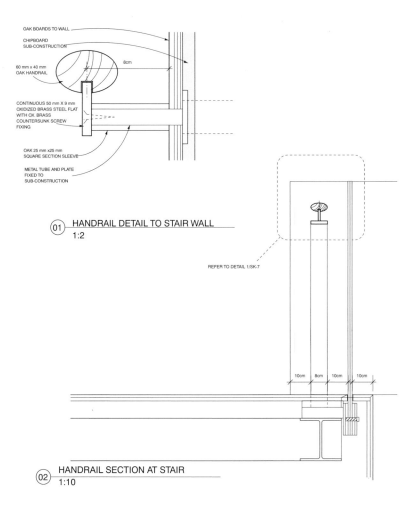

OAK BOARDS TO WALL

CHIPBOARD
SUB-CONSTRUCTION

60 mm x 40 mm
OAK HANDRAIL

8cm

CONTINUOUS 50 MM X 9 mm
OXIDIZED BRASS STEEL FLAT
WITH OX. BRASS
COUNTERSUNK SCREW
FIXING

OAK 25 mm x25 mm
SQUARE SECTION SLEEVE

METAL TUBE AND PLATE
FIXED TO
SUB-CONSTRUCTION

01 — HANDRAIL DETAIL TO STAIR WALL
1:2

REFER TO DETAIL 1/SK-7

10cm   8cm   10cm   10cm

02 — HANDRAIL SECTION AT STAIR
1:10

Craig Bassam Studio, Bally Store, Berlin, 2001. Standard European oak flooring wraps the surfaces of the store in boards that are 125 centimeters long by 10 centimeters wide and laid out in a precise pattern by a cabinetmaker.

Craig Bassam Studio, Bally Store, Berlin, 2001. The unfinished wood is oiled to enhance its natural grain and fragrance.

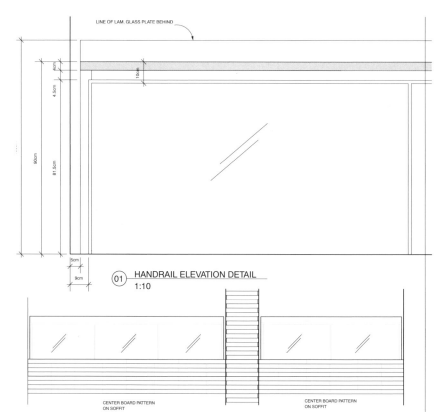

REFER TO DETAIL 1/SK-7

100cm

90cm

REFER TO FIXING DETAIL #110.01

10cm   10cm   8cm

CONFIRM DIMENSIONS

2.5cm

10cm   0.75cm

OAK CELING SLATS PARALLEL TO FLOOR BOARDS

LONG 10cm WIDE END BOARD WITH SOLID EDGES

2.5cm

10cm

OAK CELING SLATS PARALLEL TO FLOOR BOARDS

LONG 10cm WIDE END BOARD WITH SOLID EDGES

CONFIRM DIMENSION
SHOULD ALIGN WITH GROUND FLOOR MIRROR

(01) HANDRAIL AT SOFFIT SECTION
1:10

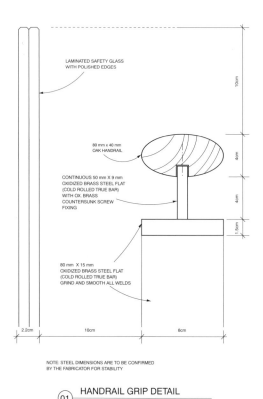

LAMINATED SAFETY GLASS WITH POLISHED EDGES

10cm

80 mm x 40 mm OAK HANDRAIL

4cm

CONTINUOUS 50 mm X 9 mm OXIDIZED BRASS STEEL FLAT (COLD ROLLED TRUE BAR) WITH OX. BRASS COUNTERSUNK SCREW FIXING

4cm

1.5cm

80 mm X 15 mm OXIDIZED BRASS STEEL FLAT (COLD ROLLED TRUE BAR) GRIND AND SMOOTH ALL WELDS

2.2cm   10cm   8cm

NOTE: STEEL DIMENSIONS ARE TO BE CONFIRMED BY THE FABRICATOR FOR STABILITY

(01) HANDRAIL GRIP DETAIL

LINE OF LAM. GLASS PLATE BEHIND

4cm

10cm

4.5cm

90cm

81.5cm

5cm

9cm

(01) HANDRAIL ELEVATION DETAIL
1:10

CENTER BOARD PATTERN ON SOFFIT

CENTER BOARD PATTERN ON SOFFIT

(02) HANDRAIL ELEVATION DETAIL
1:50

Eric J. Cobb Architect, Bruckner House, Widbey Island, Washington, 1999. The house is organized around two perpendicular board-formed concrete walls that contrast with the lightness of the flush-trimmed openings of smooth vertical grain fir.

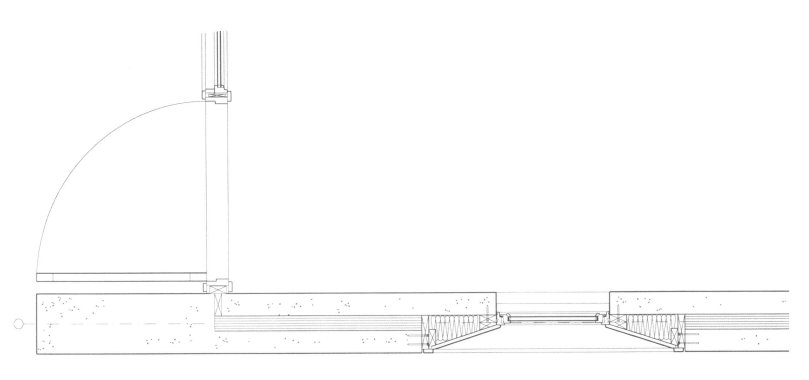

3
A6.0   PLAN DETAIL @ CONC WALL

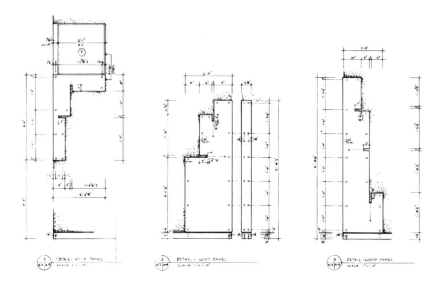

George Ranalli Architect, K-Loft, New York, 1995. Programmatic elements in the larger space of the loft are made of plaster, translucent glass, and clad at the corners in panels of birch plywood cut to irregular profiles and affixed with a pattern of screw fasteners.

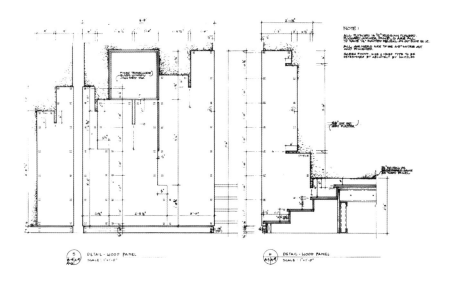

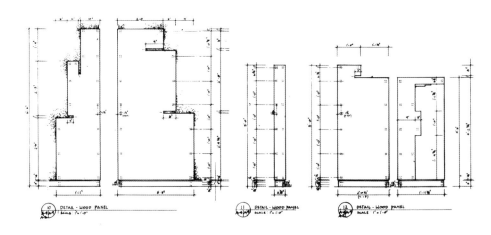

Resolution: 4 Architecture, Moody Residence, New York, 1998. Maple woodwork wraps the central core of the kitchen and unifies the surrounding spaces with built-in cabinetry and custom elements such as a chair and dining table.

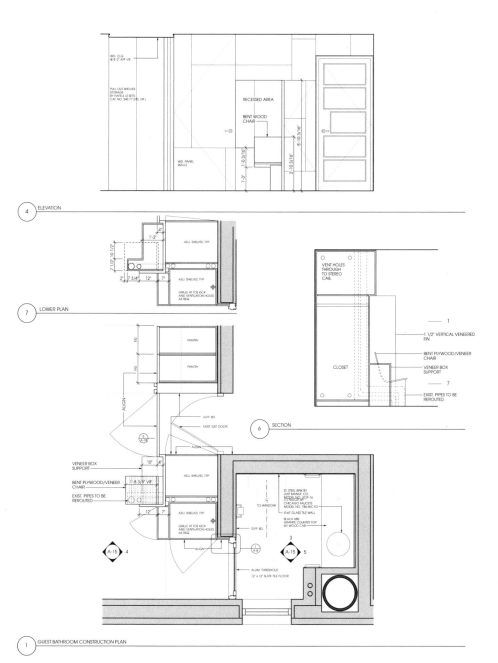

WD. CLG. @ 8'-2" AFF VIF.

PULL OUT SHELVES STORAGE BY HAFELE (2 SETS) CAT. NO. 546.77.270, VIF.)

RECESSED AREA

BENT WOOD CHAIR

WD. PANEL WALLS

5'-10 3/16"

1'-0 3/16"

2'-10 3/16"

1'-3"

④ ELEVATION

4"

1'-2"

7 1/2" 10 1/2"

ADJ. SHELVES, TYP.

2' 7 3/4" 12" 7"

ADJ. SHELVES, TYP.

GRILLE AT TOE KICK AND VENTILATION HOLES AS REQ.

⑦ LOWER PLAN

PANTRY

PANTRY

VENT HOLES THROUGH TO STEREO CAB.

CLOSET

ALIGN

GYP. BD.

EXIST. EXIT DOOR

ALIGN

VENEER BOX SUPPORT

BENT PLYWOOD/VENEER CHAIR

EXIST. PIPES TO BE REROUTED

ADJ. SHELVES, TYP.

1'-8 3/8" VIF

10" 4"

ALIGN

12" 7"

ADJ. SHELVES, TYP.

GRILLE AT TOE KICK AND VENTILATION HOLES AS REQ.

GYP. BD.

TO WINDOW

ST. STEEL SINK BY JUST MANUF. CO. MODEL NO. UCF-16 CHICAGO FAUCETS MODEL NO. 786-WC-E3

4"x4" GLASS TILE WALL

BLACK ABE GRANITE COUNTER TOP W/ WOOD CAB.

A-15 4

A-15 5

ALUM. THRESHOLD 12" x 12" SLATE TILE FLOOR

① GUEST BATHROOM CONSTRUCTION PLAN

1 1/2" VERTICAL VENEERED FIN

BENT PLYWOOD/VENEER CHAIR

VENEER BOX SUPPORT

EXIST. PIPES TO BE REROUTED

⑥ SECTION

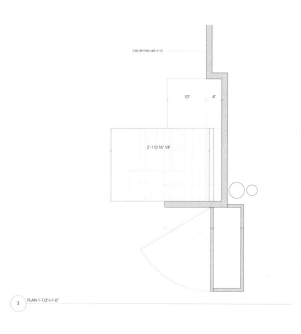

CAB. BEYOND (SEE A-15)

10" 4"

2'-1 5/16" VIF

③ PLAN 1-1/2"=1'-0"

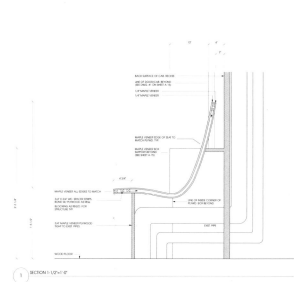

BACK SURFACE OF CAB. RECESS

LINE OF DOOR/CAB. BEYOND (SEE DWG. #1 ON SHEET A-15)

1/4" MAPLE VENEER

1/4" MAPLE VENEER

MAPLE VENEER EDGE OF SEAT TO MATCH PLYWD.

MAPLE VENEER BOX SUPPORT BEYOND (SEE SHEET A-15)

MAPLE VENEER ALL EDGES TO MATCH

3/4" X 3/4" WD. SPACER STRIPS, BOND W/ PLYWOOD AS REQ. BLOCKING AS REQ'D. FOR STRUCTUE TYP

LINE OF INSIDE CORNER OF PLYWD. BOX BEYOND

3/4" MAPLE PLYWOOD TIGHT TO EXIST PIPES

EXIST. PIPE

WOOD FLOOR

① SECTION 1-1/2"=1'-0"

Machado and Silvetti Associates, Back Bay Residence, Boston, 1992. The apartment's fireplace comprises panels of satinwood, angled and detailed to reveal that each is a veneer, not solid wood.

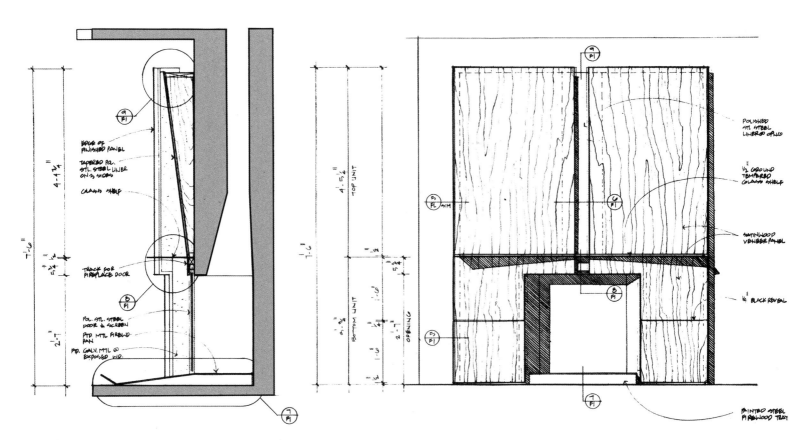

concrete

"You can have a conversation with concrete . . . the beauty of what you create comes if you honor the material for what it really is," said Louis Kahn. ■ Known to the French as *beton brut*, concrete has a raw authenticity. ■ Responsible for such ancient wonders as the Pantheon, the material was a favorite among pioneer architects of the early twentieth century, mainly because of its roots as a staple of industrial building. ■ It came into its own as masters like Saarinen, Nervi, and Candela pushed its structural limits and rendered soaring, memorable forms. ■ Brutal and beautiful.

Previous spread: Olson Sundberg Kundig Allen Architects, Mission Hill Family Estate Winery, Westbank, British Columbia, Canada, 2001. This spread: Patkau Architects, Vancouver House, Vancouver, Canada, 2000. To improve its seismic strength, the house was constructed almost entirely with reinforced, cast-in-place concrete, including the raised lap pool and its terraces. The exterior surfaces are of exposed, board-formed concrete that is textured by the formwork's rough-sawn hemlock planks. The upper level is clad with horizontal wooden louvers that deflect sunlight as it enters a set of skylights located above the principal living spaces.

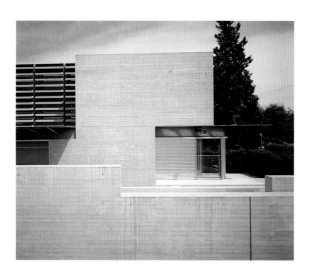

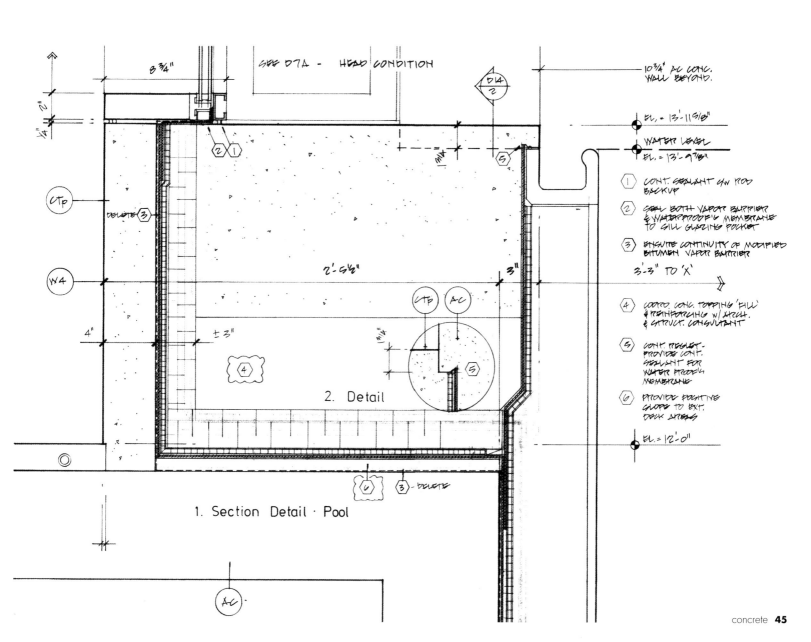

1. Section Detail · Pool

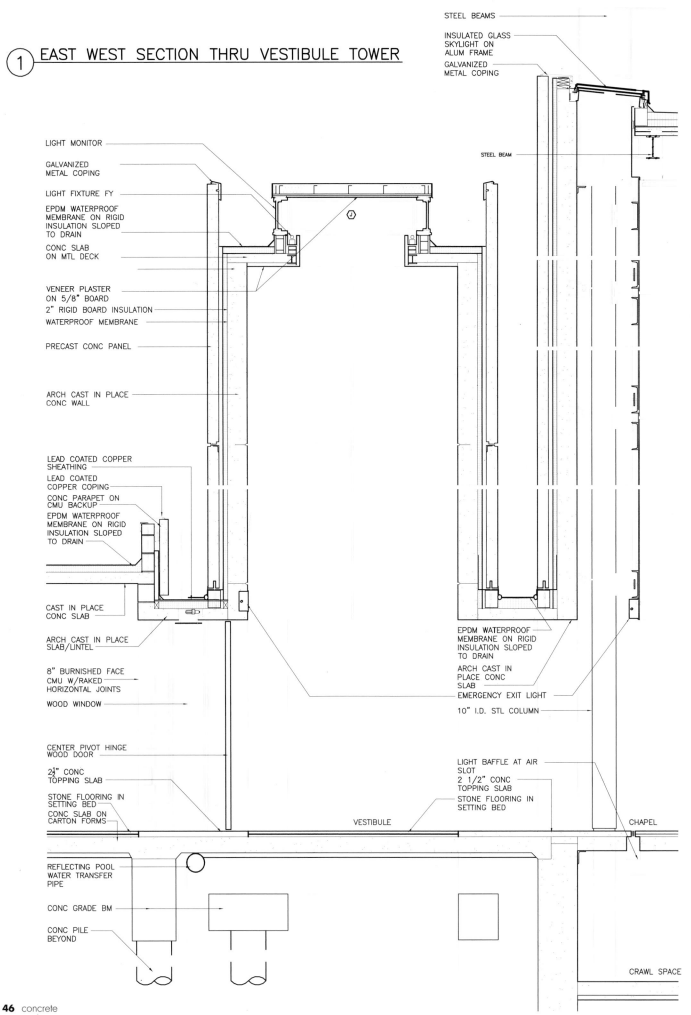

1 EAST WEST SECTION THRU VESTIBULE TOWER

STEEL BEAMS

INSULATED GLASS
SKYLIGHT ON
ALUM FRAME

GALVANIZED
METAL COPING

STEEL BEAM

LIGHT MONITOR

GALVANIZED
METAL COPING

LIGHT FIXTURE FY

EPDM WATERPROOF
MEMBRANE ON RIGID
INSULATION SLOPED
TO DRAIN

CONC SLAB
ON MTL DECK

VENEER PLASTER
ON 5/8" BOARD

2" RIGID BOARD INSULATION

WATERPROOF MEMBRANE

PRECAST CONC PANEL

ARCH CAST IN PLACE
CONC WALL

LEAD COATED COPPER
SHEATHING

LEAD COATED
COPPER COPING

CONC PARAPET ON
CMU BACKUP

EPDM WATERPROOF
MEMBRANE ON RIGID
INSULATION SLOPED
TO DRAIN

CAST IN PLACE
CONC SLAB

ARCH CAST IN PLACE
SLAB/LINTEL

8" BURNISHED FACE
CMU W/RAKED
HORIZONTAL JOINTS

WOOD WINDOW

CENTER PIVOT HINGE
WOOD DOOR

2½" CONC
TOPPING SLAB

STONE FLOORING IN
SETTING BED

CONC SLAB ON
CARTON FORMS

REFLECTING POOL
WATER TRANSFER
PIPE

CONC GRADE BM

CONC PILE
BEYOND

EPDM WATERPROOF
MEMBRANE ON RIGID
INSULATION SLOPED
TO DRAIN

ARCH CAST IN
PLACE CONC
SLAB

EMERGENCY EXIT LIGHT

10" I.D. STL COLUMN

LIGHT BAFFLE AT AIR
SLOT

2 1/2" CONC
TOPPING SLAB

STONE FLOORING IN
SETTING BED

VESTIBULE

CHAPEL

CRAWL SPACE

Previous spread: François de Menil, Architect, the Byzantine Fresco Chapel Museum, Houston, 1997. Precast concrete panels form the volume of the museum, which houses two thirteenth-century frescoes. This spread: François de Menil, Architect, Byzantine Fresco Chapel Museum, Houston, 1997. The concrete panels have mitered edges and open joints between them.

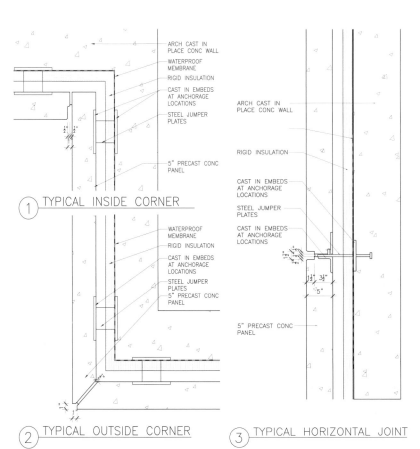

ARCH CAST IN
PLACE CONC WALL

WATERPROOF
MEMBRANE

RIGID INSULATION

CAST IN EMBEDS
AT ANCHORAGE
LOCATIONS

STEEL JUMPER
PLATES

5" PRECAST CONC
PANEL

① TYPICAL INSIDE CORNER

WATERPROOF
MEMBRANE

RIGID INSULATION

CAST IN EMBEDS
AT ANCHORAGE
LOCATIONS

STEEL JUMPER
PLATES

5" PRECAST CONC
PANEL

② TYPICAL OUTSIDE CORNER

ARCH CAST IN
PLACE CONC WALL

RIGID INSULATION

CAST IN EMBEDS
AT ANCHORAGE
LOCATIONS

STEEL JUMPER
PLATES

CAST IN EMBEDS
AT ANCHORAGE
LOCATIONS

5" PRECAST CONC
PANEL

③ TYPICAL HORIZONTAL JOINT

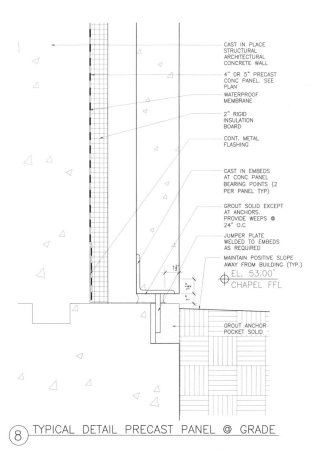

CAST IN PLACE
STRUCTURAL
ARCHITECTURAL
CONCRETE WALL

4" OR 5" PRECAST
CONC PANEL. SEE
PLAN

WATERPROOF
MEMBRANE

2" RIGID
INSULATION
BOARD

CONT. METAL
FLASHING

CAST IN EMBEDS
AT CONC PANEL
BEARING POINTS (2
PER PANEL TYP)

GROUT SOLID EXCEPT
AT ANCHORS.
PROVIDE WEEPS @
24" O.C

JUMPER PLATE
WELDED TO EMBEDS
AS REQUIRED

MAINTAIN POSITIVE SLOPE
AWAY FROM BUILDING (TYP.)

EL. 53.00'
CHAPEL FFL

GROUT ANCHOR
POCKET SOLID

⑧ TYPICAL DETAIL PRECAST PANEL @ GRADE

Steven Holl Architects, Chapel of St. Ignatius, Seattle, 1997. The chapel's exterior surfaces were created through a tilt-up construction method. Integral color concrete slabs were cast flat in twenty-one panels on the ground, raised vertically into place, and each of the hooks was capped with bronze covers.

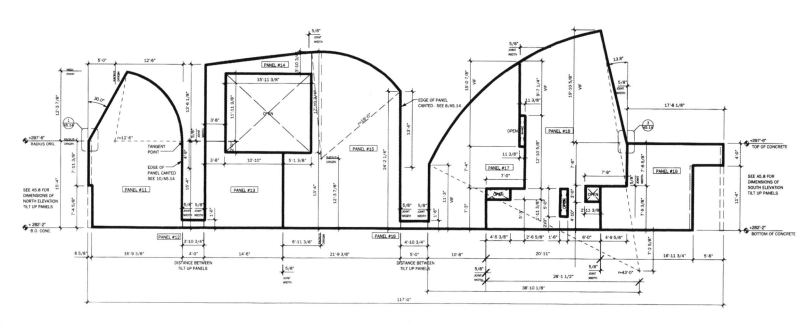

Steven Holl Architects, Texas Stretto House, Dallas, 1992. The regularity of the house's running bond pattern of concrete block contrasts markedly with the supple curvature of cast glass and arching metal roofs.

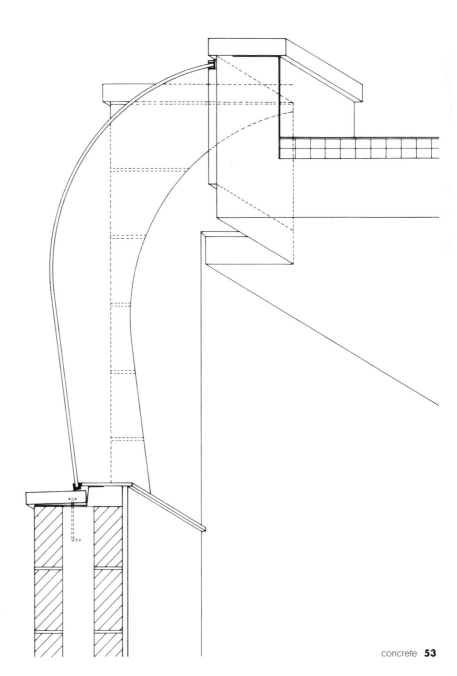

Steven Holl Architects with Vito Acconci, Storefront for Art and Architecture, New York, 1993. Using a structural concrete board, the façade of this gallery opens with hinged panels that are framed with metal reveals and fastened with exposed screw-heads.

Barkow Leibinger Architects, Trumpf Customer and Training Center, Farmington, Connecticut, 1999. Sandblasted concrete blocks with laser-cut stainless steel inserts line the interior workspaces, which are enclosed by double-height glass walls that are supported by steel frames with tension rod stiffeners.

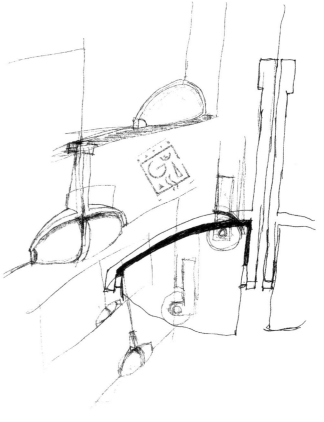

Olson Sundberg Kundig Allen Architects, Studio House, Seattle, 1998. The kitchen island is formed from a single precast concrete counter and sink, as well as operable concrete cabinet doors with bronze rollers that match tracks arcing across the concrete floor.

Olson Sundberg Kundig Allen Architects, Mission Hill Family Estate Winery, Westbank, British Columbia, Canada, 2001. An oculus punctured in the vaulted concrete ceiling provides the only natural light to the below-grade wine cellar. Following spread: Olson Sundberg Kundig Allen Architects, Mission Hill Family Estate Winery, Westbank, British Columbia, Canada, 2001. The underground cellars of the winery are blasted from the native rock and enclosed with a concrete vaulting system.

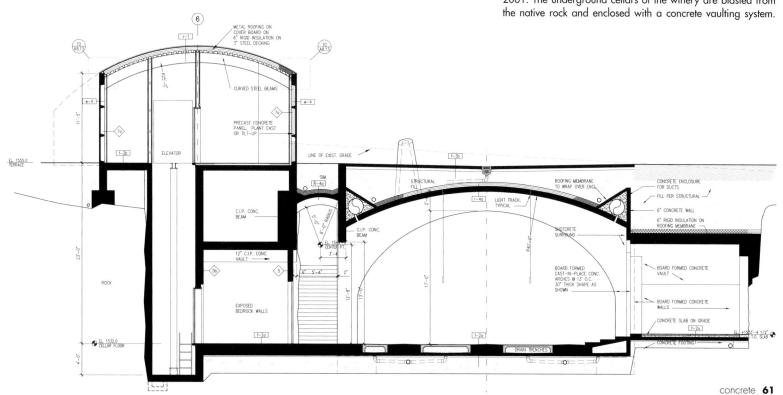

Rafael Viñoly Architects, Princeton University Stadium, Princeton, New Jersey, 1998. The stadium's double-tiered concourse is located beneath precast concrete bleachers, which allow light to pass through a grid of openings between each row of seating.

stone

The idea of stone as the essential architectural material is epitomized by the character Howard Roark in Ayn Rand's novel *The Fountainhead*: "These rocks . . . waiting to be split, ripped, pounded, reborn; waiting for the shape my hands will give them . . ." ■ The architect as primal sculptor, working in granite, limestone, and marble, forms a large part of the profession's lore. ■ The artistic aspirations and form-giving instincts are still alive. ■ But most modern stone materials are actually composites whose texture, strength, and porosity retain much of the rich character of original stone.

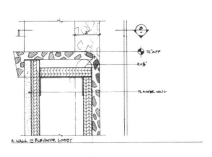

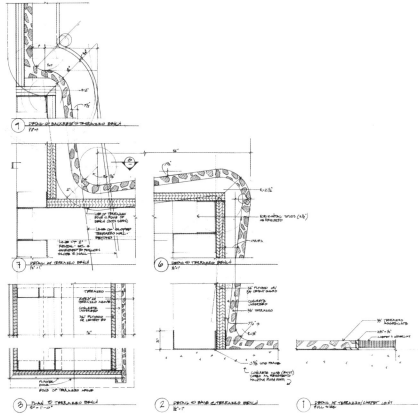

Lippincott & Margulies

Previous spread: Architecture Research Office, SoHo Loft, New York, 1999. This spread: Machado and Silvetti Associates, Lippincott & Margulies, New York, 1998. The office's material palette includes wood, perforated aluminum, blackened steel, glass, and a terrazzo wall that wraps down to form a bench, continues into the entry area as flooring, and turns upward to form a reception desk.

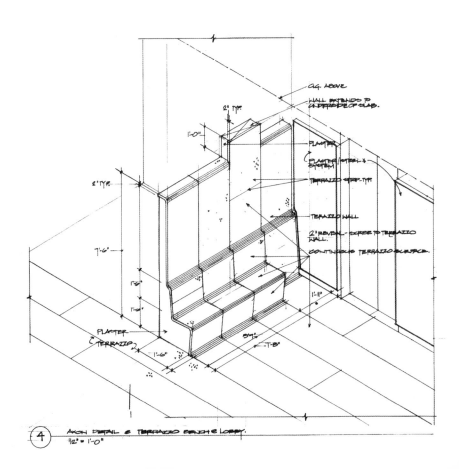

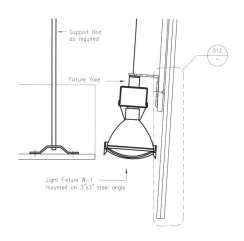

Previous spread: Gabellini Associates, Jil Sander Showroom, Milan, 2000. The floors and staircase are made of Arria limestone from Spain. This spread: Smith-Miller + Hawkinson Architects, Corning Museum of Glass, Phase One, Corning, New York, 1998. the auditorium is lined with grey-green serpentine granite and a combination of white maple and pear veneer paneling.

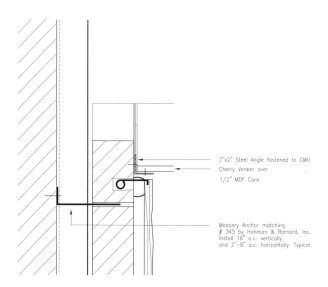

Support Rod as required

Fixture Yoke

Light Fixture W-1 mounted on 3"x3" steel angle

D8 Detail — Cove Lighting
3"=1'-0"

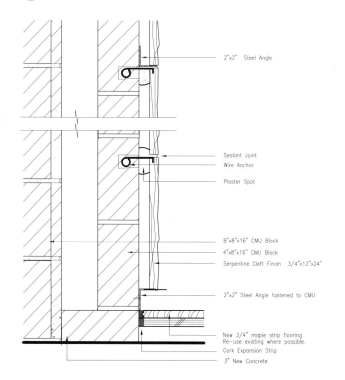

2"x2" Steel Angle fastened to CMU
Cherry Veneer over
1/2" MDF Core

Masonry Anchor matching
345 by Hohman & Barnard, Inc.
Install 16" o.c. vertically
and 2'-8" o.c. horizontally. Typical

D7 Detail —
3"=1'-0"

2"x2" Steel Angle

Sealant Joint
Wire Anchor

Plaster Spot

8"x8"x16" CMU Block
4"8"x16" CMU Block
Serpentine Cleft Finish 3/4"x12"x24"

2"x2" Steel Angle fastened to CMU

New 3/4" maple strip flooring
Re-use existing where possible.
Cork Expansion Strip
3" New Concrete

Architecture Research Office, SoHo Loft, New York, 1999. The book-matching of deeply veined blue Bahia granite creates a ten-foot-high dividing wall between a dining area and kitchen.

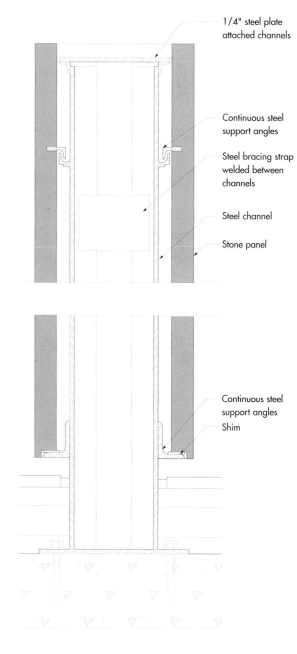

1/4" steel plate attached channels

Continuous steel support angles

Steel bracing strap welded between channels

Steel channel

Stone panel

Continuous steel support angles
Shim

Architecture Research Office, SoHo Loft, New York, 1999. A slate deflector panel reflects light from the bathroom's window across the shower wall's striated surface of black cleft slate.

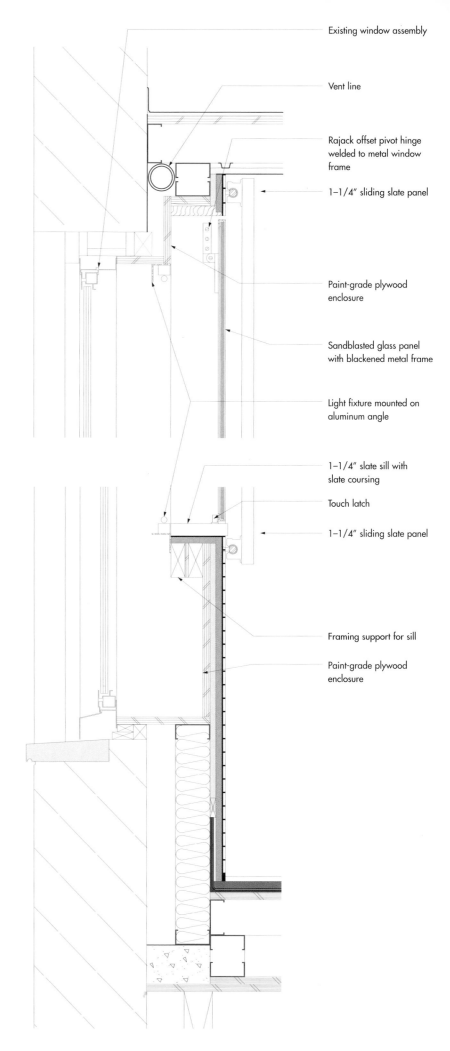

Existing window assembly

Vent line

Rajack offset pivot hinge welded to metal window frame

1–1/4" sliding slate panel

Paint-grade plywood enclosure

Sandblasted glass panel with blackened metal frame

Light fixture mounted on aluminum angle

1–1/4" slate sill with slate coursing

Touch latch

1–1/4" sliding slate panel

Framing support for sill

Paint-grade plywood enclosure

Krueck & Sexton Architects, Stainless Steel Apartment, Chicago, 1994. The polished brown soaking tub and wall rest on a terrazzo floor and stand adjacent to a sandblasted glass wall that admits light to the bathroom from the apartment's living quarters.

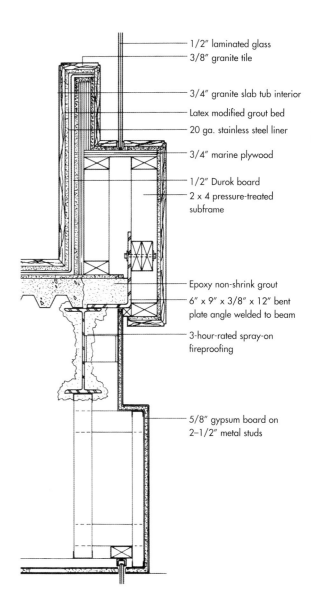

1/2" laminated glass
3/8" granite tile
3/4" granite slab tub interior
Latex modified grout bed
20 ga. stainless steel liner
3/4" marine plywood
1/2" Durok board
2 x 4 pressure-treated subframe
Epoxy non-shrink grout
6" x 9" x 3/8" x 12" bent plate angle welded to beam
3-hour-rated spray-on fireproofing
5/8" gypsum board on 2-1/2" metal studs

metal

Carl Sandberg said, "A bar of steel—it is only smoke at the heart of it, smoke and the blood of a man." ■ Born in fiery crucibles from Youngstown to Yokohoma, steel and other architectural metals form the backbone of modern architects' capabilities to build ever higher, more daring and expressive structures. ■ The innumerable surfaces and colors of building metals and their ability to be milled to minutely exacting tolerances provide designers with infinite range. ■ "For me, metal is the material of our time," said Frank Gehry. "It enables architecture to become sculpture."

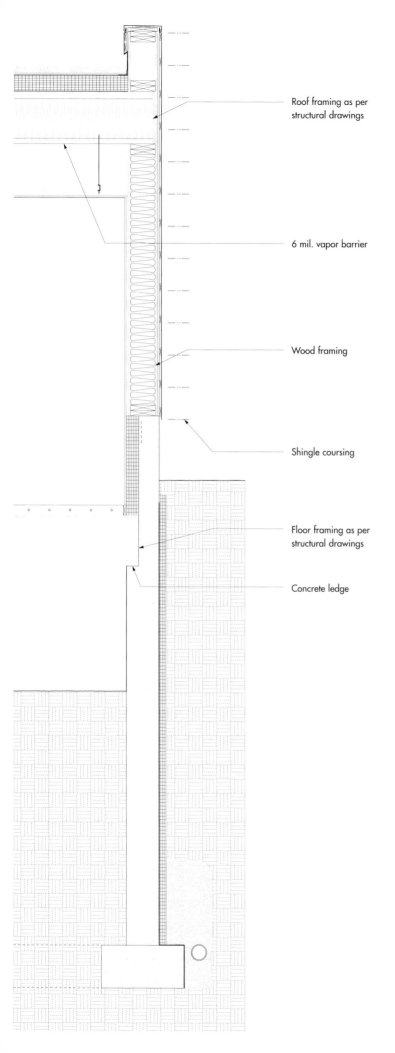

Roof framing as per
structural drawings

6 mil. vapor barrier

Wood framing

Shingle coursing

Floor framing as per
structural drawings

Concrete ledge

Previous spread: Steven Holl Architects, Texas Stretto House, Dallas, 1992. This spread: Architecture Research Office, Colorado House, Telluride, Colorado, 1999. The house's walls are parallel bands in plan, wrapped on the exterior in cor-ten shingles and resting on a foundation of sandblasted concrete. The pattern varies depending upon the orientation of each shingle and the amount of overlap between rows.

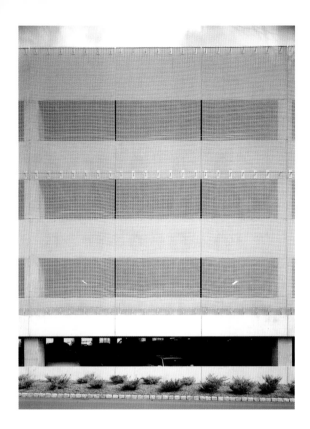

TEN Arquitectos, Princeton Parking Garage, Princeton, New Jersey, 2000. Horizontal rods and woven vertical cables form a stainless steel curtain that sheathes the outside of the garage.

Steven Holl Architects, Sarphatistraat Offices, Amsterdam, 2000. Facing a canal, the pavilion has two skins—an outer perforated screen of prepatinated copper and an inner stucco layer with patterned fields of intense colors.

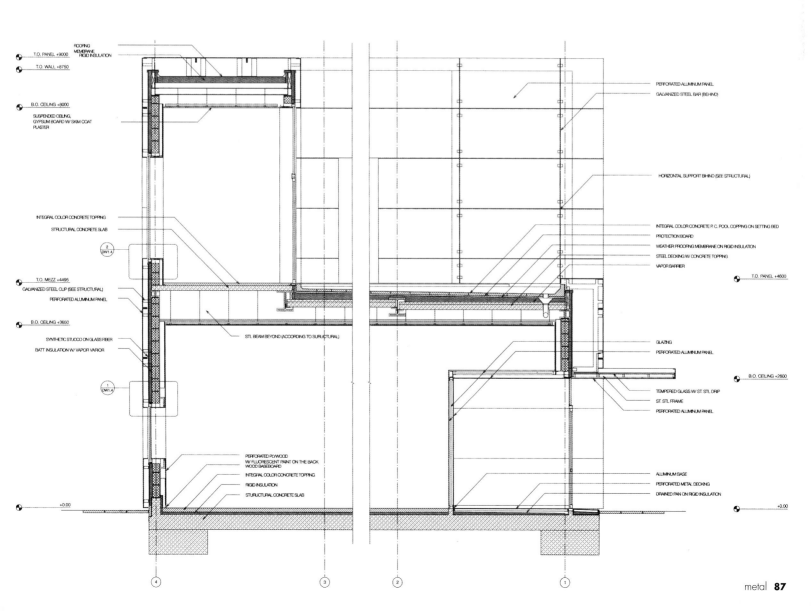

Steven Holl Architects, Makuhari Housing, Chiba, Japan, 1996. Wrapped in preweathered zinc panels, the small gatehouse cantilevers over a reflecting pool and contains a tea room. Following spread: Steven Holl Architects, Makuhari Housing, Chiba, Japan, 1996. The public meeting hall is differentiated from the larger complex by its ruddy cladding of oxidized metal.

Steven Holl Architects, Museum of Contemporary Art, Helsinki, Finland, 1998. The curved surface of the zinc roof is sliced to create skylight openings for the upper-level galleries.

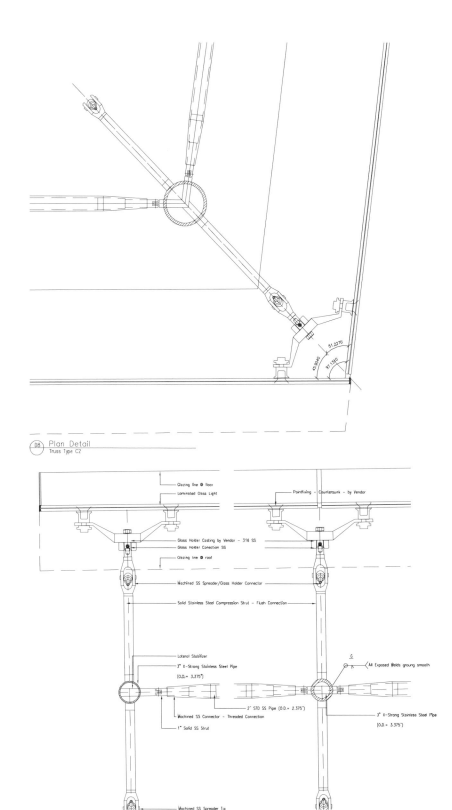

Plan Detail
Truss Type C2

Glazing line @ floor

Laminated Glass Light

Pointfixing – Countersunk – by Vendor

Glass Holder Casting by Vendor – 316 SS

Glass Holder Conection SS

Glazing line @ roof

Machined SS Spreader/Glass Holder Connector

Solid Stainless Steel Compression Strut – Flush Connection

Lateral Stabilizer

3" X-Strong Stainless Steel Pipe
(O.D.= 3.375")

All Exposed Welds ground smooth

2" STD SS Pipe (O.D.= 2.375")

Machined SS Connector – Threaded Connection

3" X-Strong Stainless Steel Pipe
(O.D.= 3.375")

1" Solid SS Strut

Machined SS Spreader Tip

Smith-Miller + Hawkinson Architects, Corning Museum of Glass, Phase Two, Corning, New York, 1999. In an effort to maintain the window wall's transparency, the glass surface is pulled away from its structural system of stainless steel tension and compression members.

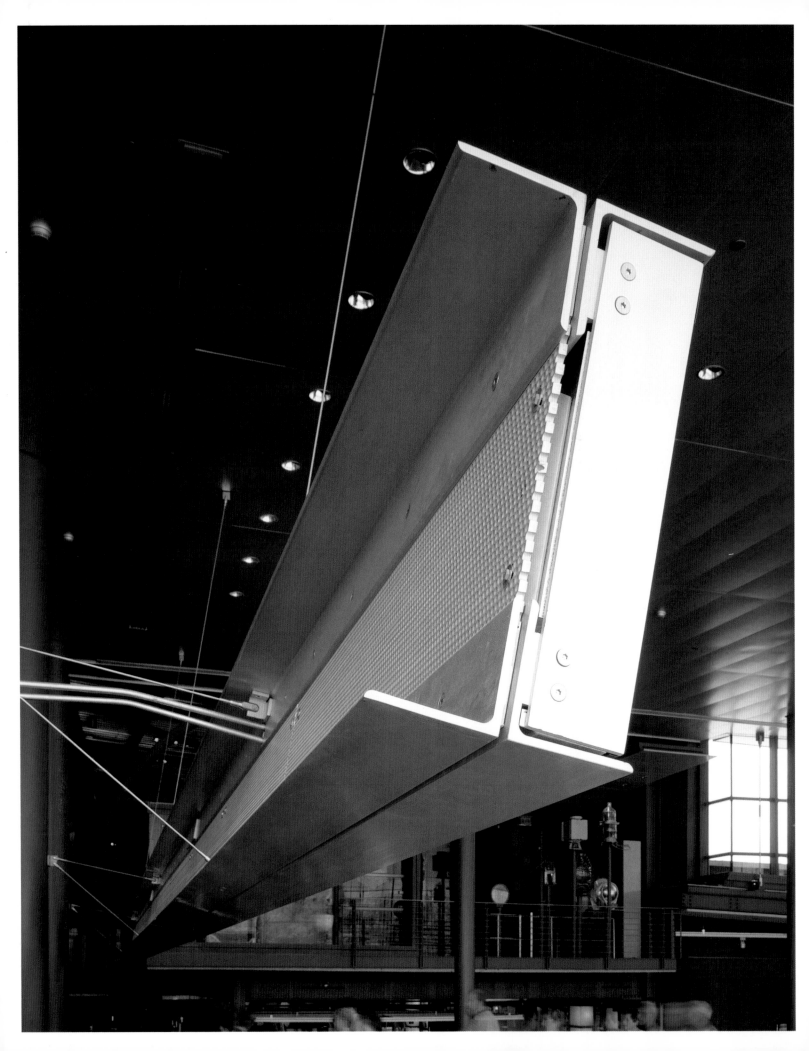

Smith-Miller + Hawkinson Architects, Corning Museum of Glass, Phase Two, Corning, New York, 1999. Supporting an LED display, a construct of anodized aluminum angles is itself suspended from the ceiling by steel cabling.

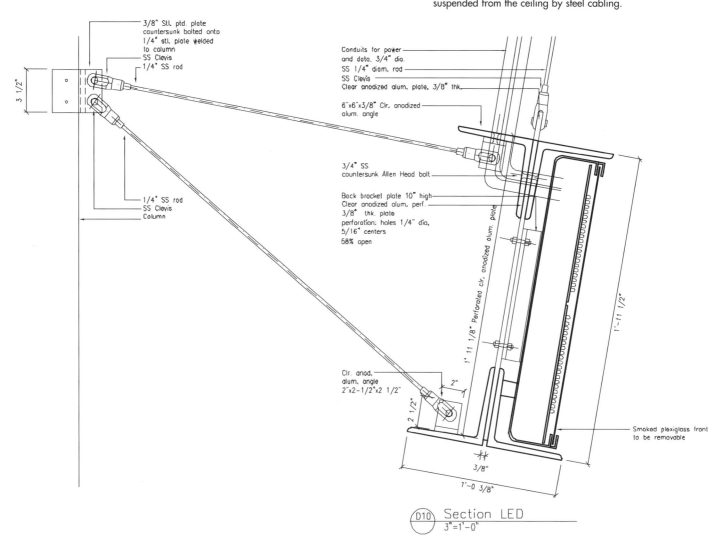

3/8" Stl. ptd. plate
countersunk bolted onto
1/4" stl. plate welded
to column
SS Clevis
1/4" SS rod

3 1/2"

1/4" SS rod
SS Clevis
Column

Conduits for power
and data, 3/4" dia.
SS 1/4" diam. rod
SS Clevis
Clear anodized alum. plate, 3/8" thk.

6"x6"x3/8" Clr. anodized
alum. angle

3/4" SS
countersunk Allen Head bolt

Back bracket plate 10" high
Clear anodized alum. perf.
3/8" thk. plate
perforation: holes 1/4" dia,
5/16" centers
58% open

1'-11 1/8" Perforated clr. anodized alum. plate

1'-11 1/2"

Clr. anod.
alum. angle
2"x2-1/2"x2 1/2"

2"

2 1/2"

Smoked plexiglass front
to be removable

3/8"

1'-0 3/8"

D10 Section LED
3"=1'-0"

Smith-Miller + Hawkinson Architects, Rotunda Gallery, Brooklyn, New York, 1993. The handrails are fabricated with anodized aluminum plates that are infilled with both clear and translucent Lexan panels.

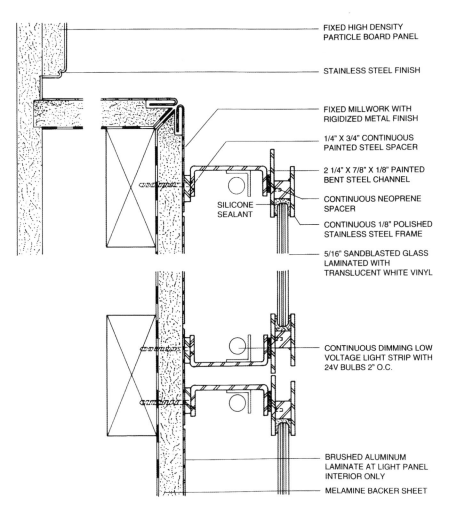

FIXED HIGH DENSITY
PARTICLE BOARD PANEL

STAINLESS STEEL FINISH

FIXED MILLWORK WITH
RIGIDIZED METAL FINISH

1/4" X 3/4" CONTINUOUS
PAINTED STEEL SPACER

2 1/4" X 7/8" X 1/8" PAINTED
BENT STEEL CHANNEL

CONTINUOUS NEOPRENE
SPACER

CONTINUOUS 1/8" POLISHED
STAINLESS STEEL FRAME

5/16" SANDBLASTED GLASS
LAMINATED WITH
TRANSLUCENT WHITE VINYL

SILICONE
SEALANT

CONTINUOUS DIMMING LOW
VOLTAGE LIGHT STRIP WITH
24V BULBS 2" O.C.

BRUSHED ALUMINUM
LAMINATE AT LIGHT PANEL
INTERIOR ONLY

MELAMINE BACKER SHEET

Krueck & Sexton Architects, Stainless Steel Apartment, Chicago, 1994. The metal-clad divider between the study and dining area supports a light-panel of sandblasted glass framed by polished stainless steel. The adjacent stair's stainless steel treads cantilever from a single stringer, floating above an ebony platform at its base.

Archi-Tectonics, Wooster Street Loft, New York, 1998. The stainless steel lower cabinets in the kitchen are complemented by cantilevering counters, one which is fixed-in-place black waterproof cement, the other which pivots and is made of custom-poured non-toxic epoxy.

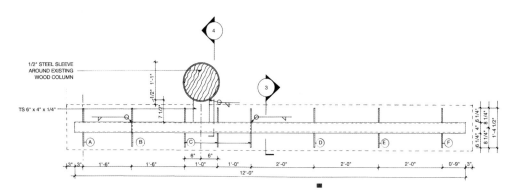

1/2" STEEL SLEEVE AROUND EXISTING WOOD COLUMN

TS 6" x 4" x 1/4"

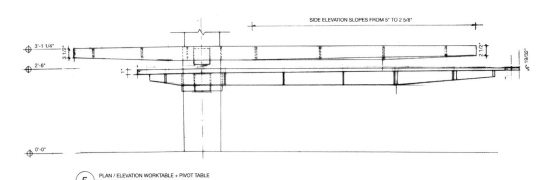

SIDE ELEVATION SLOPES FROM 5" TO 2 5/8"

5 PLAN / ELEVATION WORKTABLE + PIVOT TABLE
1" = 1'-0"

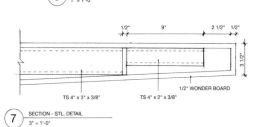

TS 4" x 3" x 3/8"   TS 4" x 2" x 3/8"   1/2" WONDER BOARD

7 SECTION - STL. DETAIL
3" = 1'-0"

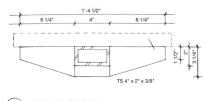

TS 4" x 2" x 3/8"

8 SECTION - STL. STRUCTURE
3" = 1'-0"

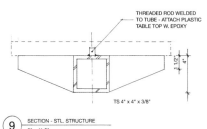

THREADED ROD WELDED TO TUBE - ATTACH PLASTIC TABLE TOP W. EPOXY

TS 4" x 4" x 3/8"

9 SECTION - STL. STRUCTURE
3" = 1'-0"

Rockwell Group, Artist Studio, New York, 1997. The sliding display wall conceals recessed shelving behind perforated metal panels. A blackened steel ledge and small magnets allow for constant change in the display of artwork and drawings.

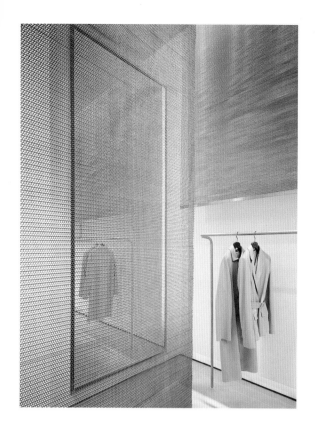

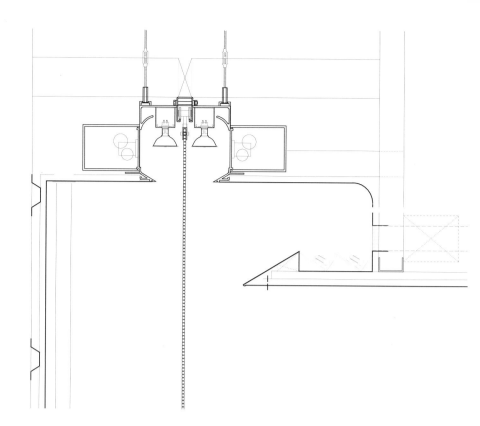

Gabellini Associates, Salvatore Ferragamo Boutique SoHo, New York, 2001. A suspended plane of nickel-silver chain mail backdrops and screens the store's clothing displays and counters.

Frank O. Gehry and Associates (with Gordon Kipping of G TECTS), TriBeCa Issey Miyake Boutique, New York, 2001. A twenty-five-foot-tall sculptural ribbon of flowing titanium occupies the heart of the store.

plaster

"There are two ways to make use of materials," said Charles Moore. "By simplifying complex forms or by enriching simple ones." ■ Plaster is an example of the latter. ■ Lathed onto an interior surface, it can take on a rich varied texture. ■ On the exterior, it can turn a building into a multi-plane medley of surfaces, light, and shadow. ■ It is a material that longs to be touched. ■ Indeed, plaster when fresh holds fast any shape pressed against it, leading Moore to call it "the material with a memory." ■ The late architect added: "The very texture of time becomes part of its enrichment."

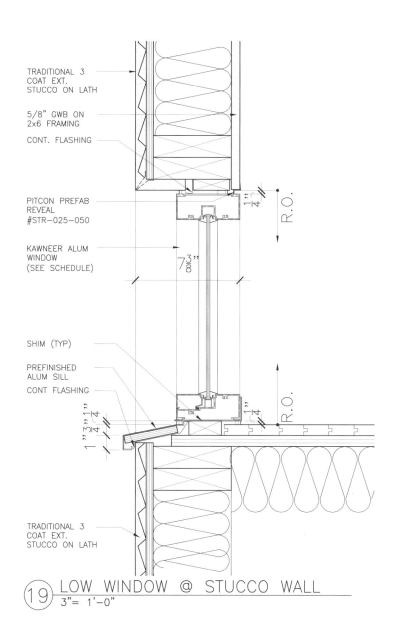

TRADITIONAL 3 COAT EXT. STUCCO ON LATH

5/8" GWB ON 2x6 FRAMING

CONT. FLASHING

PITCON PREFAB REVEAL #STR-025-050

KAWNEER ALUM WINDOW (SEE SCHEDULE)

SHIM (TYP)

PREFINISHED ALUM SILL

CONT FLASHING

TRADITIONAL 3 COAT EXT. STUCCO ON LATH

(19) LOW WINDOW @ STUCCO WALL
3" = 1'-0"

Previous spread: Olson Sundberg Kundig Allen Architects, North Seattle Residence, Seattle, 2000. This spread: François de Menil, Architect, Bank Street Residence, Houston, 2000. The house's stucco walls are overlaid with a grid of control joints and recessed aluminum windows.

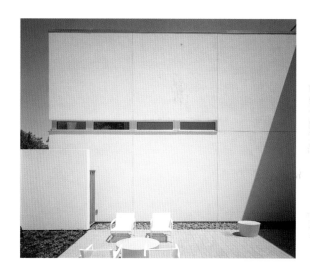

Steven Holl Architects, Museum of Contemporary Art, Helsinki, Finland, 1998. Natural light enters the galleries in a variety of ways and is diffused across the plaster surfaces by translucent glass. Following spread: Steven Holl Architects, Museum of Contemporary Art, Helsinki, Finland, 1998. The skylights are sliced into the plaster ceiling and expressed on the outer curved roof through a folded zinc plane.

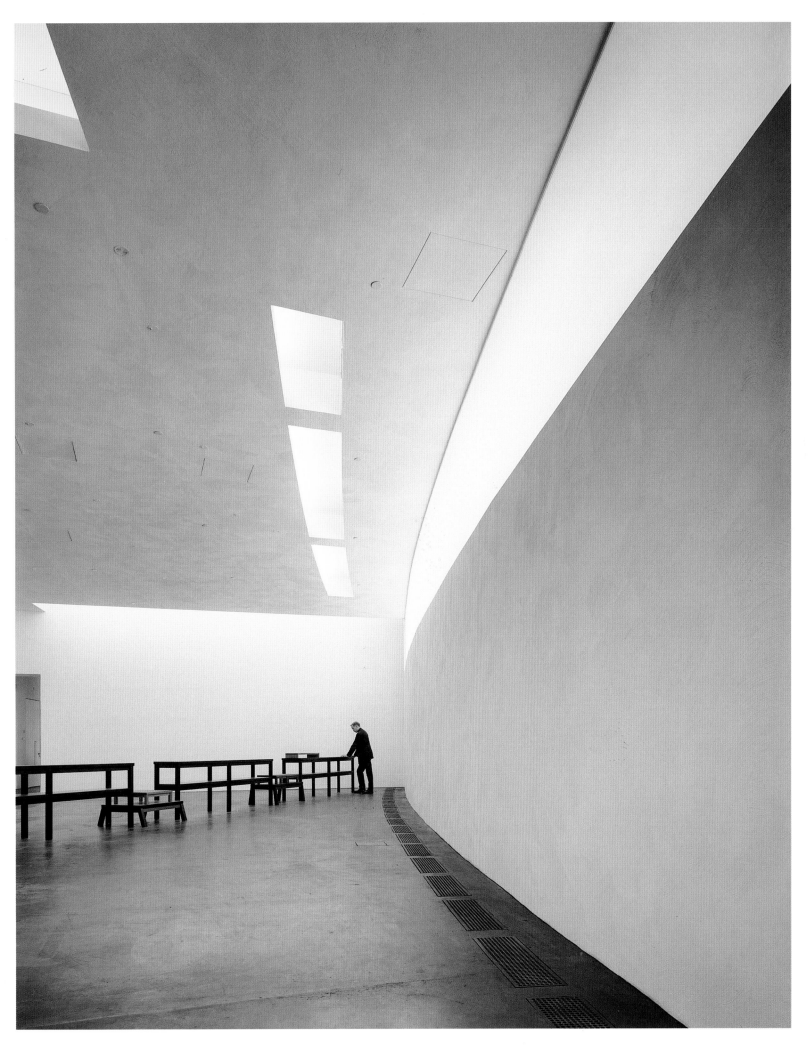

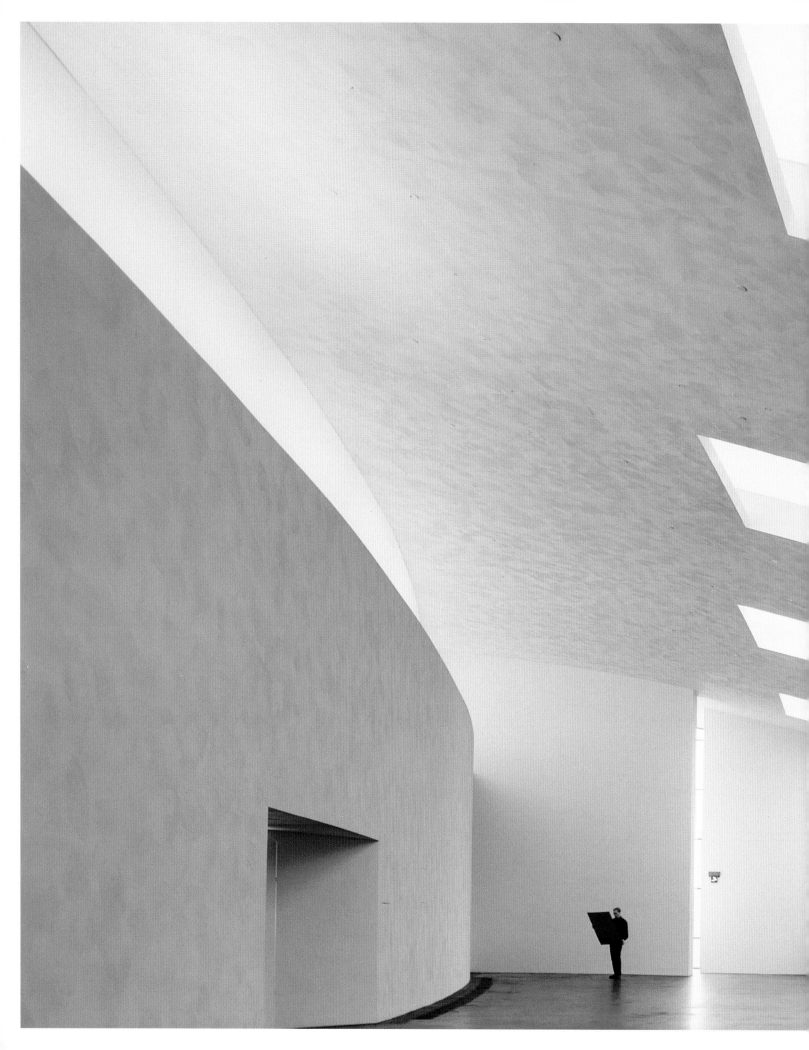

Steven Holl Architects, Museum of Contemporary Art, Helsinki, Finland, 1998. The dramatic curvature of the outside roof creates an interior plaster surface that is washed with gradations of daylight.

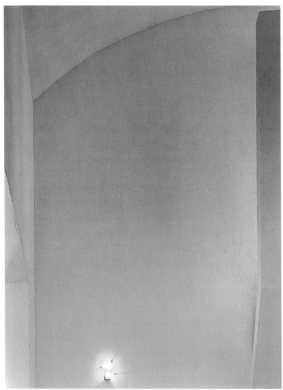

Steven Holl Architects, Chapel of St. Ignatius, Seattle, Washington, 1997. The walls of the light shafts are made of scratch-coat plaster, patterned by hand during application with large-toothed trowels and left unfinished.

Peter L. Gluck and Partners, Architects, House on Lake Michigan, Highland Park, Illinois, 1997. The dining room's vaulted ceiling is formed by layers of plywood and sheetrock, which were then finished with a steel-troweled white plaster.

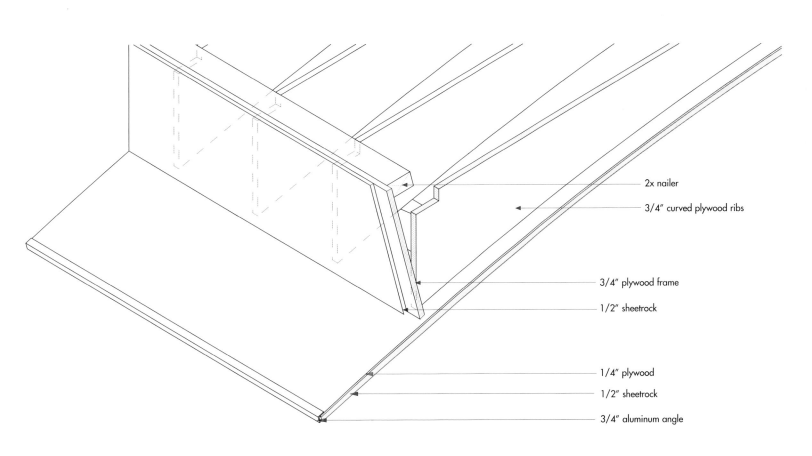

2x nailer

3/4" curved plywood ribs

3/4" plywood frame

1/2" sheetrock

1/4" plywood

1/2" sheetrock

3/4" aluminum angle

Holey Associates, Pomegranit, San Francisco, 1998. Plaster highlight walls are complemented by sliding panels composed of Lumasite, wood, or Italian veneer plaster. These allow studios and a collective space to be joined or separated.

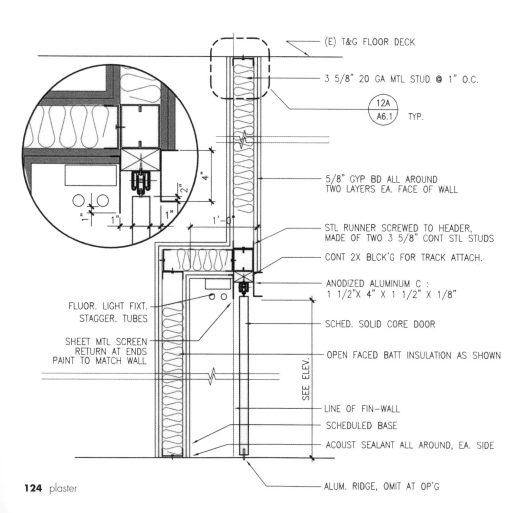

(E) T&G FLOOR DECK

3 5/8" 20 GA MTL STUD @ 1" O.C.

12A
A6.1 TYP.

5/8" GYP BD ALL AROUND
TWO LAYERS EA. FACE OF WALL

STL RUNNER SCREWED TO HEADER,
MADE OF TWO 3 5/8" CONT STL STUDS

CONT 2X BLCK'G FOR TRACK ATTACH.

ANODIZED ALUMINUM C :
1 1/2"X 4" X 1 1/2" X 1/8"

FLUOR. LIGHT FIXT.
STAGGER. TUBES

SHEET MTL SCREEN
RETURN AT ENDS
PAINT TO MATCH WALL

SCHED. SOLID CORE DOOR

OPEN FACED BATT INSULATION AS SHOWN

SEE ELEV.

LINE OF FIN-WALL

SCHEDULED BASE

ACOUST SEALANT ALL AROUND, EA. SIDE

ALUM. RIDGE, OMIT AT OP'G

Asfour Guzy Architects, T Management Offices, New York, 1999. Made from skim-coated plaster, the curvilinear form of the stairwell is based upon a deformed cylinder.

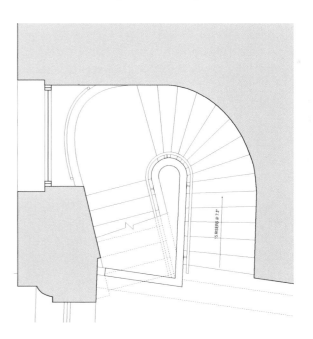

fabric

"Silently as a dream the fabric rose, no sound of hammer or of saw was there," said William Cowpor. ■ The use of the words "weaving" and "fabric" are ubiquitous in architecture. ■ And yet as an indoor and outdoor material, fabric is an anomaly among the others—soft, pliable, usable in innumerable ways. ■ Fabric placed creatively can redefine an entire space, but do so gently. ■ Like screens, fabric can add an air of mystery. ■ Fabric can be subtly translucent without being transparent, strong and taut or billowing in the breeze. ■ Part of the rich quilt of building.

Previous spread: Archi-Tectonics, Wooster Street Loft, New York, 1998. This spread: Olson Sundberg Kundig Allen Architects, Studio House, Seattle, 1998. A canvas curtain hung from a cedar track lines the board-formed concrete wall of the double-height studio space.

Previous spread: Archi-Tectonics, Wooster Street Loft, New York, 1998. Curtains of ultra-suede material complement the bedroom's warm hardwood surfaces, providing a soft counterpoint to the precision of a stainless steel and translucent glass wall system. This spread: Pasanella + Klein Stolzman + Berg Architects, Central Park Apartment, New York, 1999. Sliding panels of tightly stretched canvas on stainless steel frames conceal the bedroom's storage.

ADDITIONAL NOTES:

a. SLIDING SCREEN FRAME – 1"X1" STAINLESS STEEL TUBE CONSTRUCTION, SANDBLASTED FINISH

b. HEAVY COTTON CANVAS SCREEN – STITCHED TOGETHER

c. EDGE REINFORCED W/ 1/4" DIA. STAINLESS STEEL ROD

d. GROMMET HARDWARE

e. LEATHER STRIP BINDING

f. BARN DOOR TRACK & HANGER

g. MESH SCREEN – TO BE SPECIFIED

h. 1/4"X1/2" RECTANGULAR OPENING 4" O.C.

i. 3/16" DIA. STAINLESS STEEL CONTINUOUS ROD BENT TO SHAPE THREADED THROUGH STAINLESS STEEL TUBE AND WELDED IN PLACE

j. STAINLESS STEEL PANEL INFILL

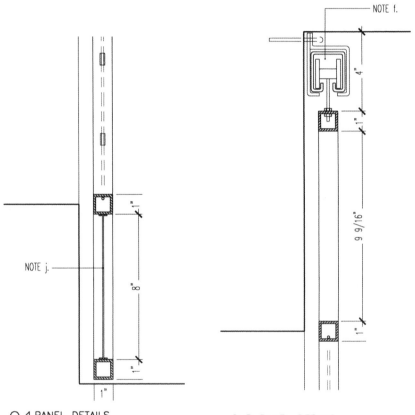

03 PANEL DETAILS
FULL SCALE

01 PANEL DETAILS
3" = 1'-0"

02 PANEL DETAILS
3" = 1'-0"

Philippe Starck, Jean Paul Gaultier, New York, 2002. Like luxuriant furnishings, the walls are faced with taffeta upholstery that is buttoned at the center of each rectangle.

Gisela Stromeyer Design, Mega Art, New York, 1998. Occupied by a printing company, this warehouse space is subdivided by custom-cut, spandex privacy screens that are suspended from metal hooks in the ceiling and made taut by rods at the floor.

Gisela Stromeyer Design, Club Incognito, Zurich, 1998. The five lanterns are made of spandex stretched with fiberglass rings.

Gisela Stromeyer Design, Club Incognito, Zurich, 1998. Suspended from the ceiling, the spandex membranes are stretched and layered in three panels above the club's bar.

Rockwell Group, Cirque du Soleil, Orlando, Florida, 1999. The tensile structure's fabric-like membrane is made from Teflon-coated fiberglass.

synthetics

It was in the post-World War II era that the full potential of plastics and other synthetic building materials became apparent. ■ In the age of Dwight Eisenhower and chrome-finned cars, designers like Charles and Ray Eames saw in synthetics things no other media could offer: malleability, durability, and the kind of cost savings only available through mass production. ■ Now new generations of designers are rendering objects in an unfathomable range of shapes, textures, and colors. ■ Synthetic materials remain as full of possibility as the era that gave them birth.

Previous spread: STUDIOS Architecture, RiskMetrics Group, New York, 1999. This spread: Turett Collaborative Architects, Tommy Boy Music, New York, 1992. In this hip-hop record label's office, the walls are composed of translucent acrylic Lumasite with visible wooden framing.

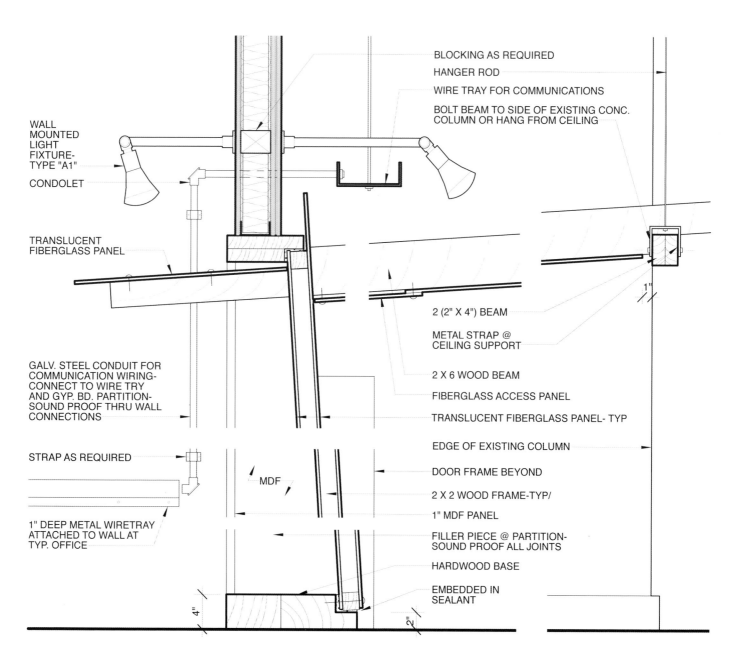

BLOCKING AS REQUIRED

HANGER ROD

WIRE TRAY FOR COMMUNICATIONS

BOLT BEAM TO SIDE OF EXISTING CONC. COLUMN OR HANG FROM CEILING

WALL MOUNTED LIGHT FIXTURE-TYPE "A1"

CONDOLET

TRANSLUCENT FIBERGLASS PANEL

2 (2" X 4") BEAM

METAL STRAP @ CEILING SUPPORT

2 X 6 WOOD BEAM

FIBERGLASS ACCESS PANEL

TRANSLUCENT FIBERGLASS PANEL- TYP

GALV. STEEL CONDUIT FOR COMMUNICATION WIRING-CONNECT TO WIRE TRY AND GYP. BD. PARTITION-SOUND PROOF THRU WALL CONNECTIONS

EDGE OF EXISTING COLUMN

DOOR FRAME BEYOND

2 X 2 WOOD FRAME-TYP/

1" MDF PANEL

STRAP AS REQUIRED

MDF

FILLER PIECE @ PARTITION-SOUND PROOF ALL JOINTS

HARDWOOD BASE

1" DEEP METAL WIRETRAY ATTACHED TO WALL AT TYP. OFFICE

EMBEDDED IN SEALANT

1"

4"

2"

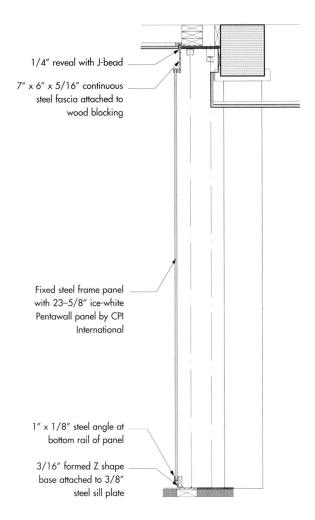

1/4" reveal with J-bead

7" x 6" x 5/16" continuous steel fascia attached to wood blocking

Fixed steel frame panel with 23–5/8" ice-white Pentawall panel by CPI International

1" x 1/8" steel angle at bottom rail of panel

3/16" formed Z shape base attached to 3/8" steel sill plate

Architecture Research Office, Capital Z Offices, New York, 1998. The office's walls are formed of extruded polycarbonate panels that are typically used in exterior skylight applications. The custom-fabricated panels have blackened steel mullions and clear sliding glass doors, which have anigre wooden inserts for handles.

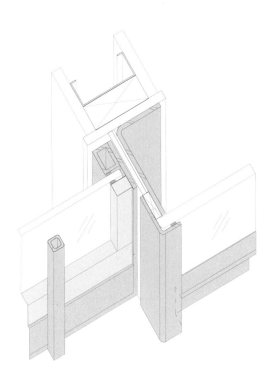

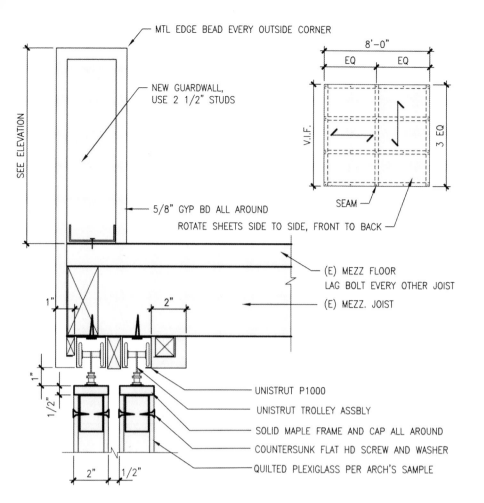

MTL EDGE BEAD EVERY OUTSIDE CORNER

NEW GUARDWALL,
USE 2 1/2" STUDS

SEE ELEVATION

5/8" GYP BD ALL AROUND

ROTATE SHEETS SIDE TO SIDE, FRONT TO BACK

8'-0"

EQ   EQ

V.I.F.

3 EQ

SEAM

(E) MEZZ FLOOR
LAG BOLT EVERY OTHER JOIST

(E) MEZZ. JOIST

1"

2"

1"

1/2"

2"   1/2"

UNISTRUT P1000

UNISTRUT TROLLEY ASSBLY

SOLID MAPLE FRAME AND CAP ALL AROUND

COUNTERSUNK FLAT HD SCREW AND WASHER

QUILTED PLEXIGLASS PER ARCH'S SAMPLE

Holey Associates, Pomegranit, San Francisco, 1998. The back-of-house functions in this post-production editing firm are screened behind sliding panels composed of two layers of Lumasite, each turned in opposite directions and framed in solid maple.

Sidnam Petrone Gartner Architects, Coty Corporate Offices, New York, 2000. Freestanding conference rooms are clad in plexi-glass and honeycomb panels, which are supported by clear-stained wooden framing.

Helfand Architecture, DoubleClick Offices, New York, 1997. Standing in contrast to workstations of heavy-grained Parallam boards, the corrugated Resolite walls provide a translucent divider between open workspaces and private rooms.

Previous spread: Office for Metropolitan Architecture/Rem Koolhaas and Architecture Research Office, Prada Store SoHo, New York, 2001. A wall and ceiling of corrugated plastic create a backdrop to suspended metal-mesh display containers and a wave-like floor of zebrawood. This spread: David Ling Architect, Cabana, New York, 1998. The office's three-story atrium and staircases are lined on one side with a waterfall that spills across a folded wall of backlit, corrugated fiberglass.

glass

"Beinahe nichts," the great modernist Ludwig Mies van der Rohe was fond of saving—"Almost nothing." ■ Glass is the ethereal "non material" which was accorded a virtual apotheosis by twentieth-century architects. ■ Glass brings the outside in, and vice versa. ■ Today designers exploit the material's diverse potential in both public and private realms. ■ Large expanses of glazing render a building open and transparent, while at the same time mystical and otherworldly. ■ Percy Bysshe Shelley: "Life, like a dome of many-colored glass, stains the white radiance of eternity."

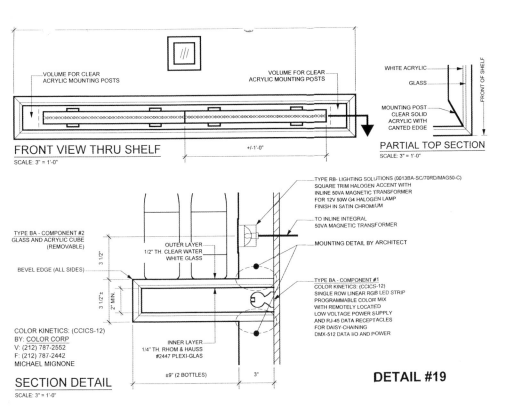

FRONT VIEW THRU SHELF
SCALE: 3" = 1'-0"

VOLUME FOR CLEAR ACRYLIC MOUNTING POSTS

VOLUME FOR CLEAR ACRYLIC MOUNTING POSTS

PARTIAL TOP SECTION
SCALE: 3" = 1'-0"

WHITE ACRYLIC

GLASS

FRONT OF SHELF

MOUNTING POST CLEAR SOLID ACRYLIC WITH CANTED EDGE

TYPE RB- LIGHTING SOLUTIONS (0013BA-SC/70RD/MAG50-C) SQUARE TRIM HALOGEN ACCENT WITH INLINE 50VA MAGNETIC TRANSFORMER FOR 12V 50W G4 HALOGEN LAMP FINISH IN SATIN CHROMIUM

TO INLINE INTEGRAL 50VA MAGNETIC TRANSFORMER

MOUNTING DETAIL BY ARCHITECT

TYPE BA - COMPONENT #1
COLOR KINETICS: (CCICS-12)
SINGLE ROW LINEAR RGB LED STRIP
PROGRAMMABLE COLOR MIX
WITH REMOTELY LOCATED
LOW VOLTAGE POWER SUPPLY
AND RJ-45 DATA RECEPTACLES
FOR DAISY-CHAINING
DMX-512 DATA I/O AND POWER

TYPE BA - COMPONENT #2
GLASS AND ACRYLIC CUBE
(REMOVABLE)

BEVEL EDGE (ALL SIDES)

OUTER LAYER
1/2" TH. CLEAR WATER
WHITE GLASS

3 1/2"

3 1/2"±
2" MIN.

COLOR KINETICS: (CCICS-12)
BY: COLOR CORP
V: (212) 787-2552
F: (212) 787-2442
MICHAEL MIGNONE

INNER LAYER
1/4" TH. RHOM & HAUSS
#2447 PLEXI-GLAS

±9" (2 BOTTLES)   3"

SECTION DETAIL
SCALE: 3" = 1'-0"

DETAIL #19

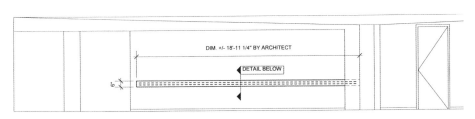

DIM. +/- 18'-11 1/4" BY ARCHITECT

DETAIL BELOW

6"

FRONT ELEVATION OF TYPE BA-1 SHELF
SCALE: 1/4" = 1'-0"

TYPE BA-1 - COMPONENT #2
GLASS AND ACRYLIC CUBE
(REMOVABLE)

OUTER LAYER
1/2" TH. CLEAR WATER
WHITE GLASS

MOUNTING DETAIL BY ARCHITECT

BEVEL EDGE (ALL SIDES)

6"

INNER LAYER
1/4" TH. RHOM & HAUSS
#2447 PLEXI-GLAS

TYPE BA-1 - COMPONENT #1
COLOR KINETICS: (CCICS-12)
TWO ROWS LINEAR RGB LED STRIP
PROGRAMMABLE COLOR MIX
WITH REMOTELY LOCATED
LOW VOLTAGE POWER SUPPLY
AND RJ-45 DATA RECEPTACLES
FOR DAISY-CHAINING
DMX-512 DATA I/O AND POWER

COLOR KINETICS: (CCICS-12)
BY: COLOR CORP
V: (212) 787-2552
F: (212) 787-2442
MICHAEL MIGNONE

DIM. BY ARCHITECT

SECTION DETAIL
SCALE: 3" = 1'-0"

DETAIL #20

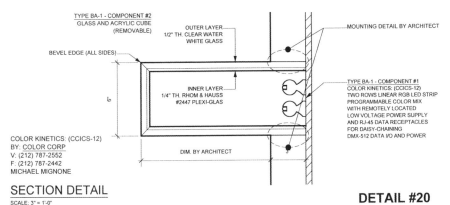

Previous spread: Davis Brody Bond, Valeo Thermal Systems, North American Headquarters and Technical Center, Auburn Hills, Michigan, 1998. This spread: Pasanella + Klein Stolzman + Berg Architects, The Shoreham Hotel, New York, 2000. Organized to draw guests through the spaces, a series of glass surfaces and volumes emit intense colors.

Archi-Tectonics, Wooster Street Loft, New York, 1998. The apartment's interior is organized by a faceted wall of stainless steel supports with panels of translucent Sumi glass.

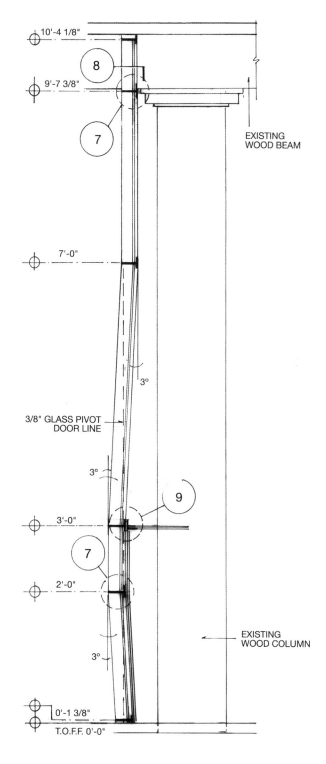

10'-4 1/8"

8

9'-7 3/8"

7

EXISTING
WOOD BEAM

7'-0"

3°

3/8" GLASS PIVOT
DOOR LINE

3°

9

3'-0"

7

2'-0"

EXISTING
WOOD COLUMN

3°

0'-1 3/8"

T.O.F.F. 0'-0"

5 SECTION
1" = 1'-0"

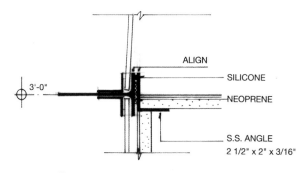

ALIGN

3'-0"

SILICONE

NEOPRENE

S.S. ANGLE
2 1/2" x 2" x 3/16"

9 DETAIL CONNECTION GLASSWALL / MASTERBATH
3" = 1'-0"

Gabellini Associates, Park Avenue Apartment, New York, 1998. The bathroom is treated as a freestanding space defined by luminous glass walls and counterbalanced by black volumes of ribbon mahogany.

Gabellini Associates, Jil Sander Showroom, Hamburg, 1997.
The water-white doors and mirrors are low-iron glass supported
by thin-profiled frames of nickel silver.

Machado and Silvetti Associates, Lippincott & Margulies, New York, 1998. Blackened steel frames support a wall comprising panels of translucent blue, clear, and sandblasted glass.

MSM Architects, USM Furniture Showroom, New York, 2002. Four layers of Starfire glass with a translucent interlayer form the stair's risers and treads, which are illuminated from inside. Following spread: MSM Architects, USM Furniture Showroom, New York, 2002. The staircase's supports are concealed and each step pulls back four inches from the tempered glass sidewall to reaffirm the sense of structural independence.

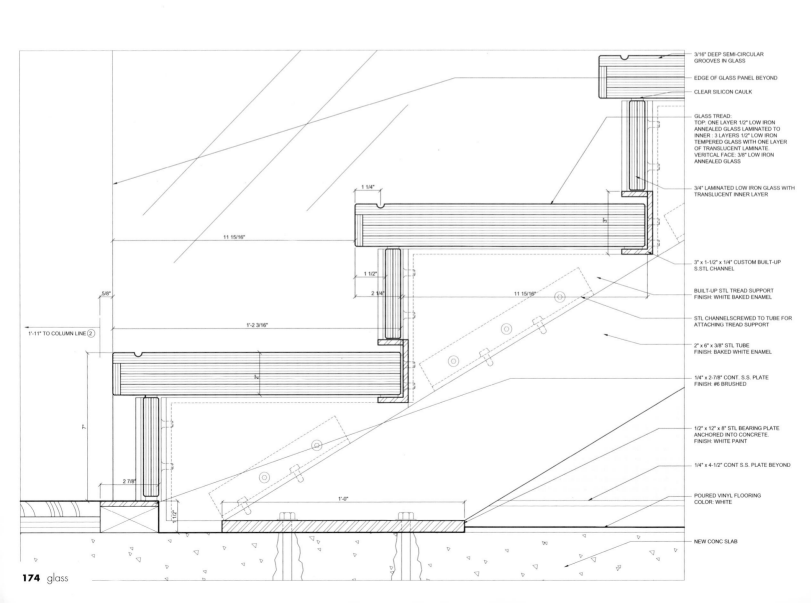

3/16" DEEP SEMI-CIRCULAR GROOVES IN GLASS

EDGE OF GLASS PANEL BEYOND

CLEAR SILICON CAULK

GLASS TREAD:
TOP: ONE LAYER 1/2" LOW IRON ANNEALED GLASS LAMINATED TO INNER : 3 LAYERS 1/2" LOW IRON TEMPERED GLASS WITH ONE LAYER OF TRANSLUCENT LAMINATE. VERITCAL FACE: 3/8" LOW IRON ANNEALED GLASS

3/4" LAMINATED LOW IRON GLASS WITH TRANSLUCENT INNER LAYER

3" x 1-1/2" x 1/4" CUSTOM BUILT-UP S.STL CHANNEL

BUILT-UP STL TREAD SUPPORT FINISH: WHITE BAKED ENAMEL

STL CHANNELSCREWED TO TUBE FOR ATTACHING TREAD SUPPORT

2" x 6" x 3/8" STL TUBE FINISH: BAKED WHITE ENAMEL

1/4" x 2-7/8" CONT. S.S. PLATE FINISH: #6 BRUSHED

1/2" x 12" x 8" STL BEARING PLATE ANCHORED INTO CONCRETE. FINISH: WHITE PAINT

1/4" x 4-1/2" CONT S.S. PLATE BEYOND

POURED VINYL FLOORING COLOR: WHITE

NEW CONC SLAB

1 1/4"

11 15/16"

1 1/2"

2 1/4"

11 15/16"

5/8"

1'-11" TO COLUMN LINE ②

1'-2 3/16"

2"

7"

2 7/8"

1'-0"

1 1/2"

Gluckman Mayner Architects, Katayone Adeli Boutique, New York, 1999. Stained plywood panels and translucent glass walls set off the dressing rooms from the remainder of the store.

Peter Marino + Assoc Architects, Chanel Store, London, 2002. The LED-lit walls and ceiling are twin layers of low-iron glass with a ceramic fritted interlayer. The display shows a faint image of the Chanel logo, and can be programmed to emit a wide array of other visual images.

Peter Marino + Assoc Architects, Chanel Store, Osaka, Japan, 2001. A low-iron clear glass curtain wall contains a white ceramic interlayer, creating an active surface illuminated by LED backlighting for changing displays of text and images.

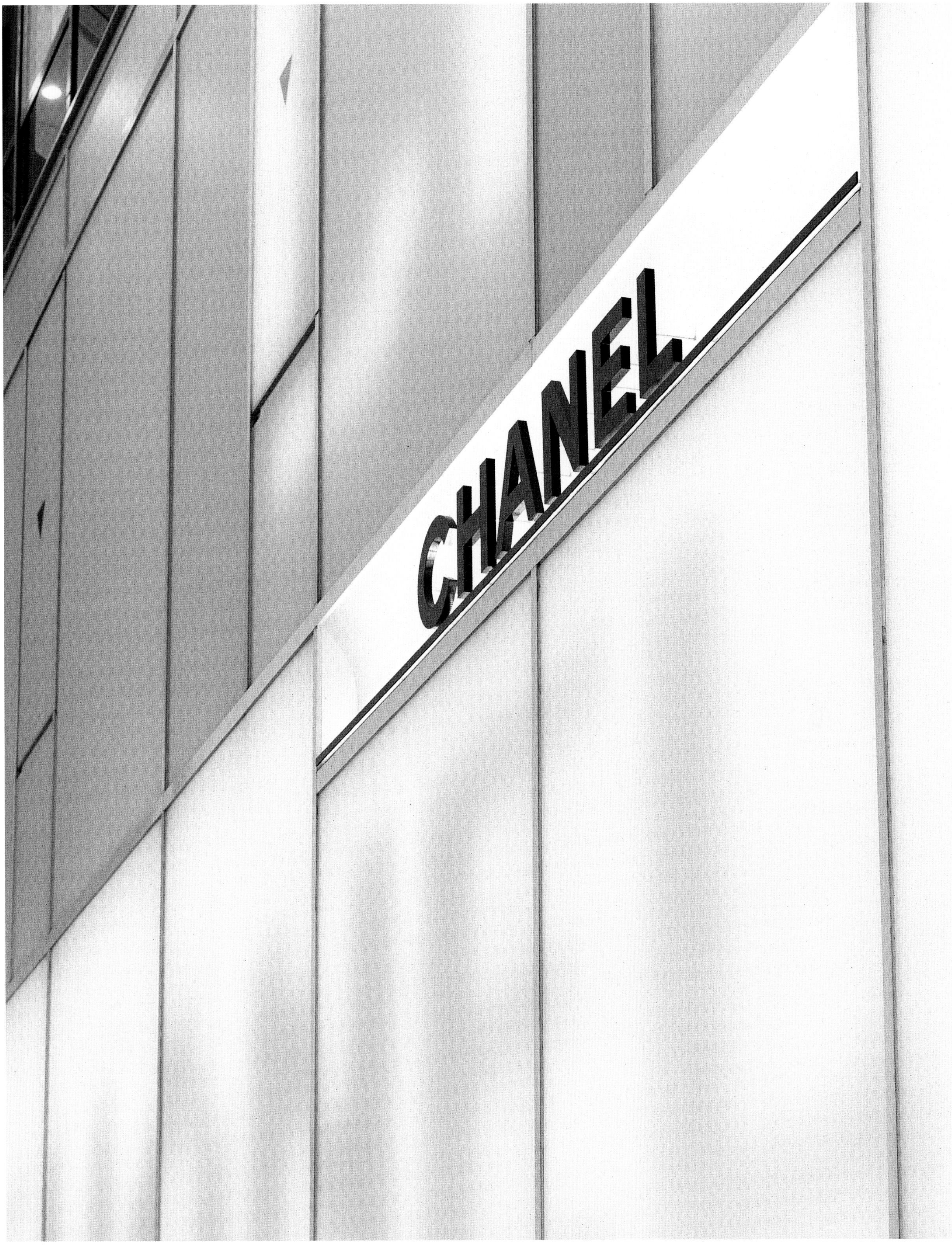
CHANEL

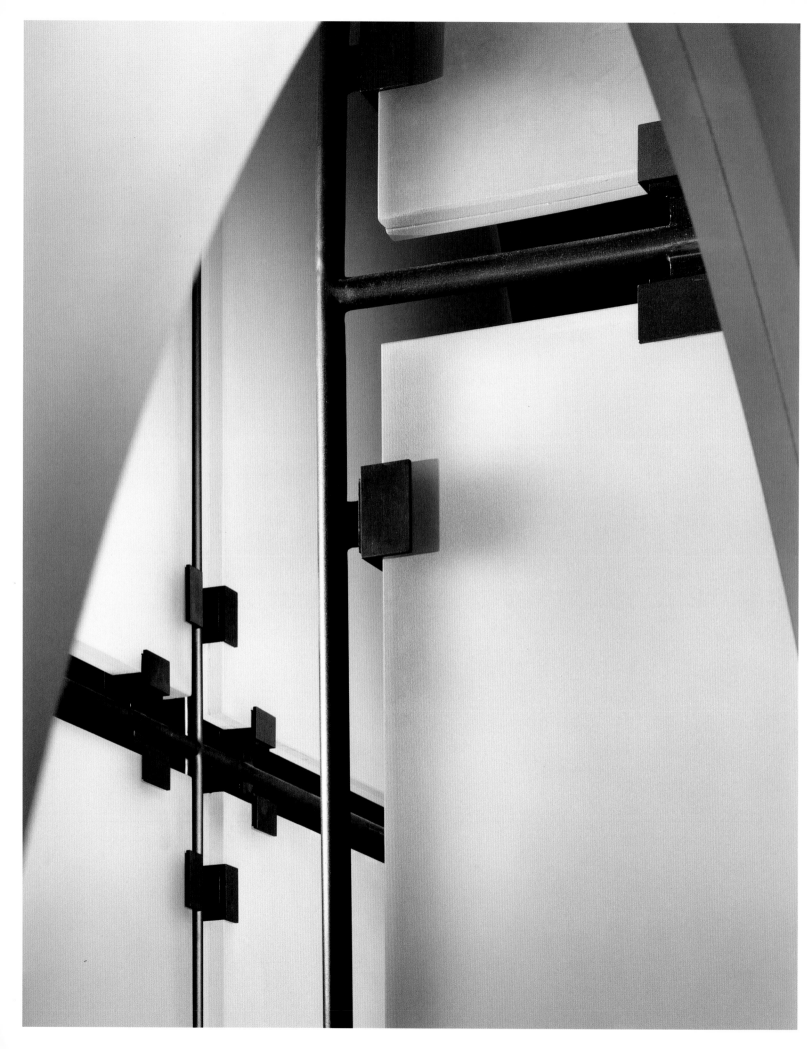

François de Menil, Architect, Byzantine Fresco Chapel Museum, Houston, 1997. Like a stage set constructed in a black box, laminated sheets of frosted glass are clipped to steel pipes, formally evoking the original setting of the frescoes on display.

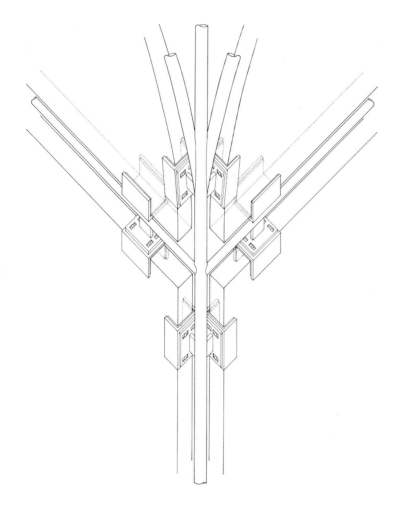

Steven Holl Architects, Chapel of St. Ignatius, Seattle, Washington, 1997. The chapel's processional route passes by the baptismal font, which is illuminated by an adjacent translucent glass panel.

Steven Holl Architects, Cranbrook Institute of Science, Bloomfield Hills, Michigan, 1999. Sunlight passes through seven types of glass in the entry vestibule's windows and skylights, creating a range of lighting effects on the interior's white plaster surfaces.

Steven Holl Architects, Bellevue Art Museum, Bellevue, Washington, 2001. The rooftop terrace's curving wall of glass planks provides light to a stair behind.

We are indebted to a large number of people whose help was indispensable in the creation of this book. At Rockport Publishers, our appreciation extends to Ken Fund and Winnie Prentiss for their enormous and unconditional support, the trust they placed in us, and the creative freedoms they allowed. Special thanks are due to Doug Dolezal for generously providing images. To James McCown and Lisa Pascarelli, we owe a substantial debt of gratitude for their willingness to be enlisted at the most strenuous moments of editing and production. Rodolfo Machado and Jorge Silvetti provided support without which this project would never have occurred. To Paul Warchol, who opened his extensive photography library to us, we cannot sufficiently express our appreciation or our respect for his work. During several trips to his studio and while sifting through thousands and thousands of images in his archives, we depended upon the kind support of Amy Barkow, Gabrielle Bendiner-Viani, Michele Convery, Bilyana Dimitrova, and Ursula Warchol. And most of all, we are indebted to the creative forces behind the details we have showcased—a list of architects and designers too numerous to recount here. Each deserves our heartfelt thanks.

acknowledgements & dedications

To Judith and Michael Pasnik, for all your gifts of love. —MP

For Lisa Pascarelli, whose friendship always exceeds the deepest meaning of this word. —ORO